ALSO BY MARJANE SATRAPI

Persepolis: The Story of a Childhood
Persepolis 2: The Story of a Return
Embroideries

CHICKEN WITH PLUMS

CHICKEN WITH PLUMS

MARJANE SATRAPI

PANTHEON BOOKS   NEW YORK

L'Association

Pantheon Books and colophon are registered trademarks of Random House, Inc.

Library of Congress Cataloging-in-Publication Data
Satrapi, Marjane, [date].
[Poulet aux prunes. English]
Chicken with plums / Marjane Satrapi.
p. cm.
ISBN 0-375-42415-6
1. Khan, Nasser Ali—Comic books, strips, etc. 2. Tar (Lute) players—Iran—Biography—Comic books, strips, etc. 3. Graphic novels. I. Title.
ML419.K495S313 2006
955.05'3092—dc22
[B] 2006043156

www.pantheonbooks.com
Printed in Canada
First American Edition

CHICKEN WITH PLUMS

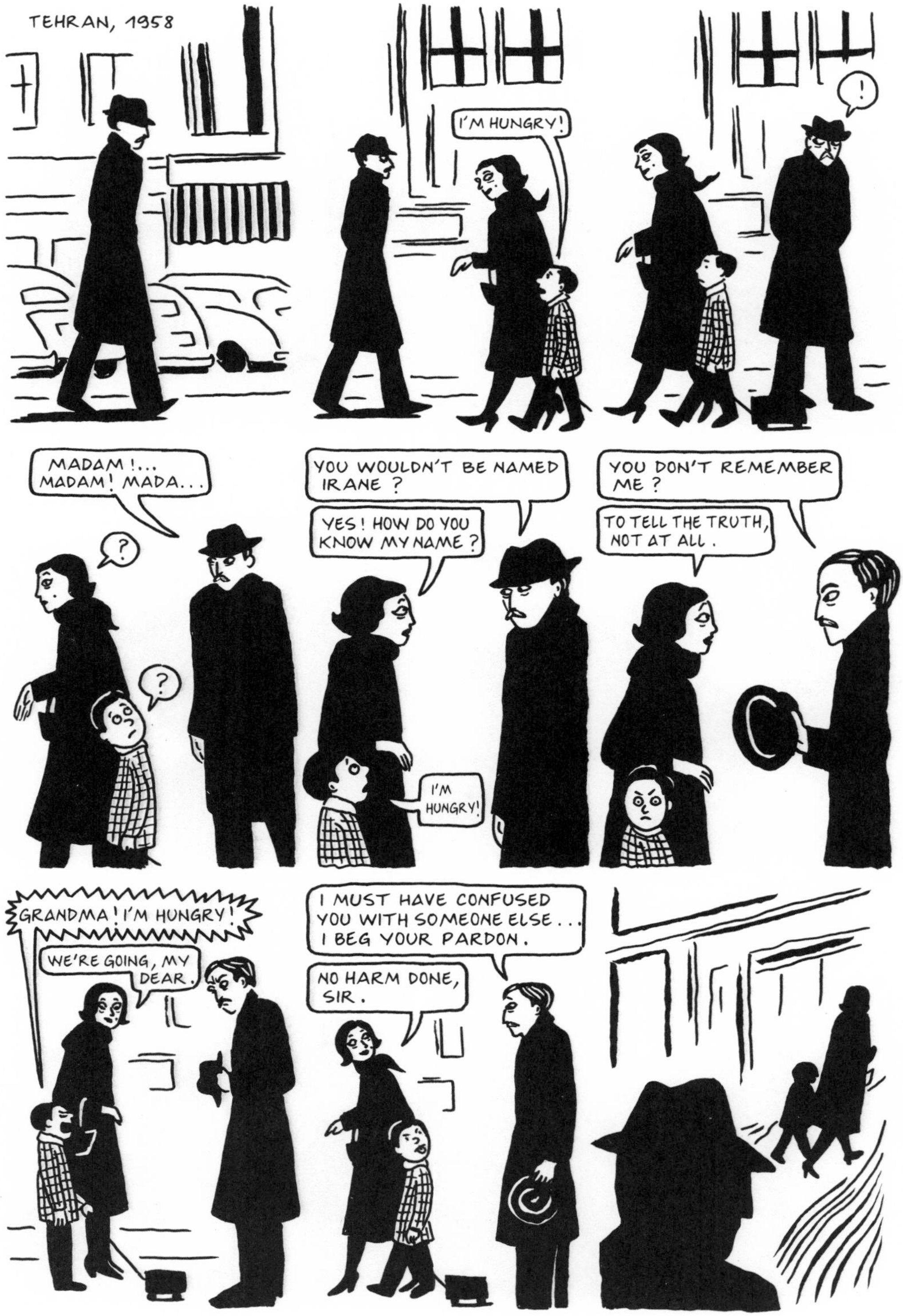
TEHRAN, 1958
I'M HUNGRY!
!
MADAM!... MADAM! MADA...
?
?
YOU WOULDN'T BE NAMED IRANE ?
YES! HOW DO YOU KNOW MY NAME ?
I'M HUNGRY!
YOU DON'T REMEMBER ME ?
TO TELL THE TRUTH, NOT AT ALL.
GRANDMA! I'M HUNGRY!
WE'RE GOING, MY DEAR.
I MUST HAVE CONFUSED YOU WITH SOMEONE ELSE... I BEG YOUR PARDON.
NO HARM DONE, SIR.

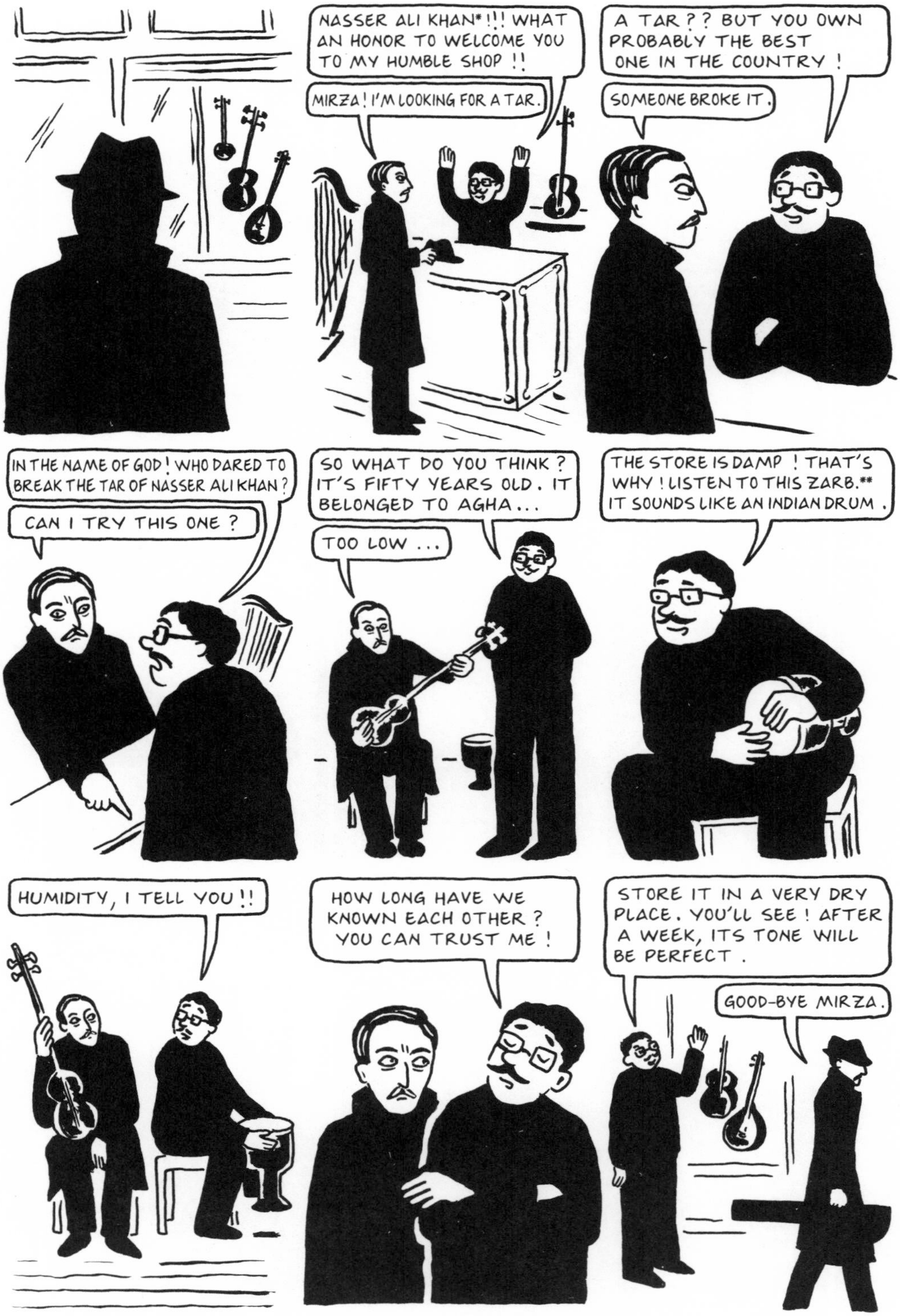
NASSER ALI KHAN*!!! WHAT AN HONOR TO WELCOME YOU TO MY HUMBLE SHOP !!
MIRZA! I'M LOOKING FOR A TAR.
A TAR ? ? BUT YOU OWN PROBABLY THE BEST ONE IN THE COUNTRY !
SOMEONE BROKE IT.
IN THE NAME OF GOD! WHO DARED TO BREAK THE TAR OF NASSER ALI KHAN?
CAN I TRY THIS ONE ?
SO WHAT DO YOU THINK ? IT'S FIFTY YEARS OLD. IT BELONGED TO AGHA...
TOO LOW ...
THE STORE IS DAMP ! THAT'S WHY ! LISTEN TO THIS ZARB.** IT SOUNDS LIKE AN INDIAN DRUM .
HUMIDITY, I TELL YOU !!
HOW LONG HAVE WE KNOWN EACH OTHER ? YOU CAN TRUST ME !
STORE IT IN A VERY DRY PLACE. YOU'LL SEE ! AFTER A WEEK, ITS TONE WILL BE PERFECT .
GOOD-BYE MIRZA.

*KHAN MEANS "LORD-SIR."

**IRANIAN PERCUSSION INSTRUMENT.

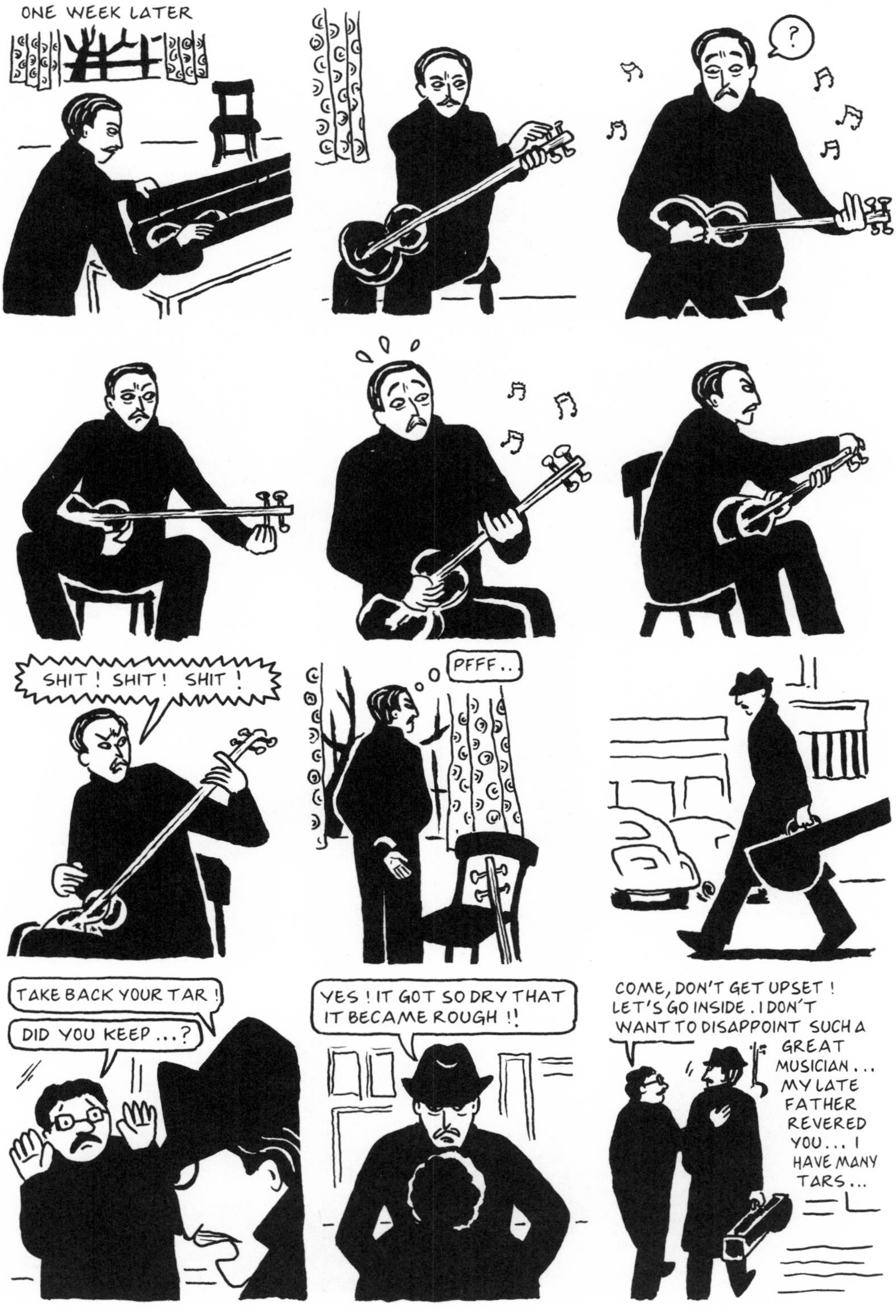
ONE WEEK LATER
?
SHIT ! SHIT ! SHIT !
PFFF..
TAKE BACK YOUR TAR !
DID YOU KEEP ...?
YES ! IT GOT SO DRY THAT IT BECAME ROUGH !!
COME, DON'T GET UPSET ! LET'S GO INSIDE. I DON'T WANT TO DISAPPOINT SUCH A GREAT MUSICIAN... MY LATE FATHER REVERED YOU... I HAVE MANY TARS...

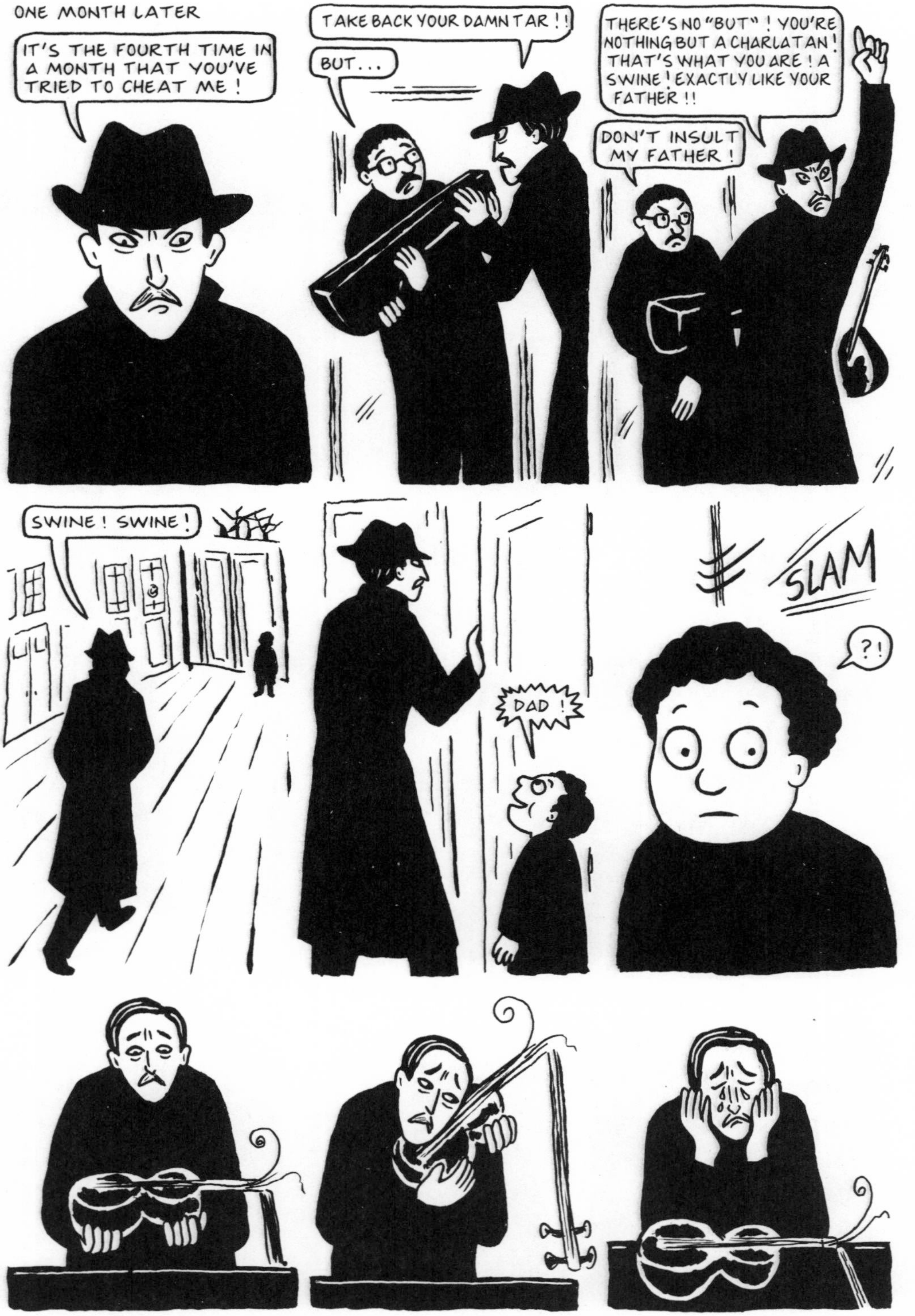
ONE MONTH LATER
IT'S THE FOURTH TIME IN A MONTH THAT YOU'VE TRIED TO CHEAT ME !
TAKE BACK YOUR DAMN TAR ! !
BUT. . .
THERE'S NO "BUT" ! YOU'RE NOTHING BUT A CHARLATAN ! THAT'S WHAT YOU ARE ! A SWINE ! EXACTLY LIKE YOUR FATHER ! !
DON'T INSULT MY FATHER !
SWINE ! SWINE !
DAD !
SLAM
?!

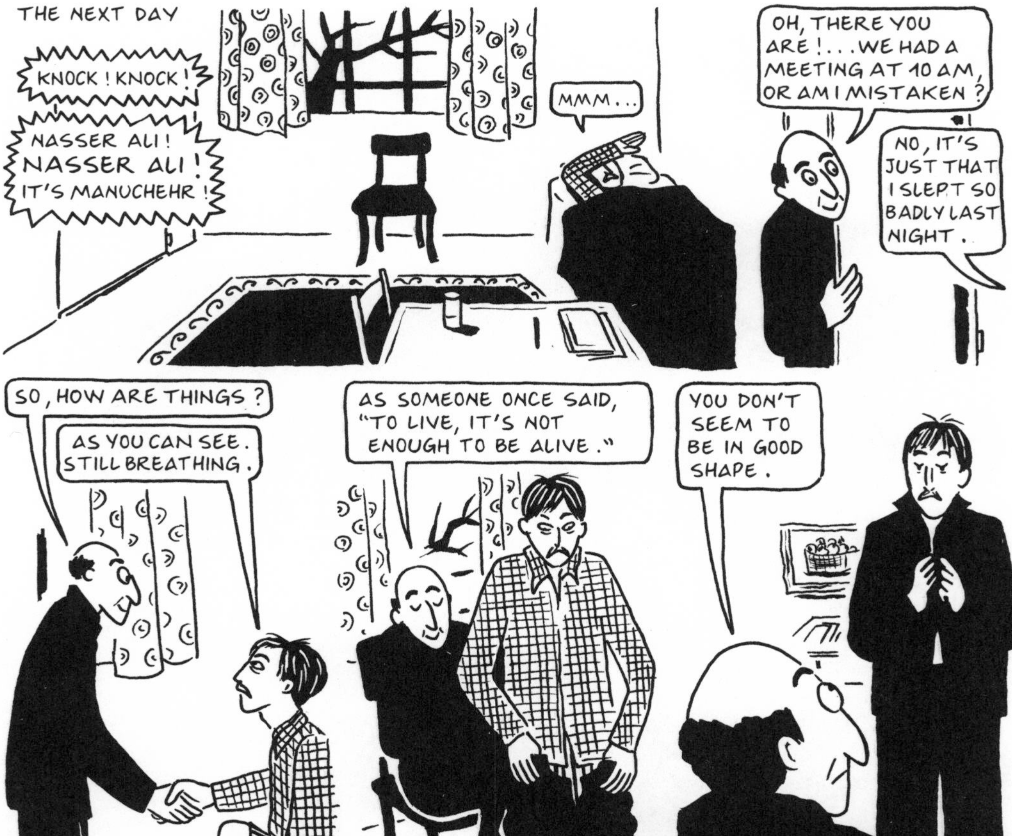
THE NEXT DAY
KNOCK! KNOCK!
NASSER ALI! NASSER ALI! IT'S MANUCHEHR!
MMM...
OH, THERE YOU ARE!... WE HAD A MEETING AT 10 AM, OR AM I MISTAKEN?
NO, IT'S JUST THAT I SLEPT SO BADLY LAST NIGHT.
SO, HOW ARE THINGS?
AS YOU CAN SEE. STILL BREATHING.
AS SOMEONE ONCE SAID, "TO LIVE, IT'S NOT ENOUGH TO BE ALIVE."
YOU DON'T SEEM TO BE IN GOOD SHAPE.
ALTHOUGH, HOW ARE YOU SUPPOSED TO FEEL GOOD WITH THINGS AS THEY ARE.
I'VE REALLY HAD THE IMPRESSION THAT SINCE THE COUP D'ÉTAT* EVERYTHING IS GETTING OUT OF HAND... WE ARE ENTERING A NEW ERA.
PERSONALLY, I HAVE LOST CONFIDENCE IN THE FUTURE.

*IN MARCH 1951, MOSSADEGH, THEN A MEMBER OF PARLIAMENT, NATIONALIZED IRAN'S OIL. IN APRIL OF THE SAME YEAR, HE WAS NAMED PRIME MINISTER. IN AUGUST 1953, MOSSADEGH WAS OUSTED IN A COUP D'ÉTAT INSTIGATED BY THE CIA WITH THE HELP OF THE BRITISH.

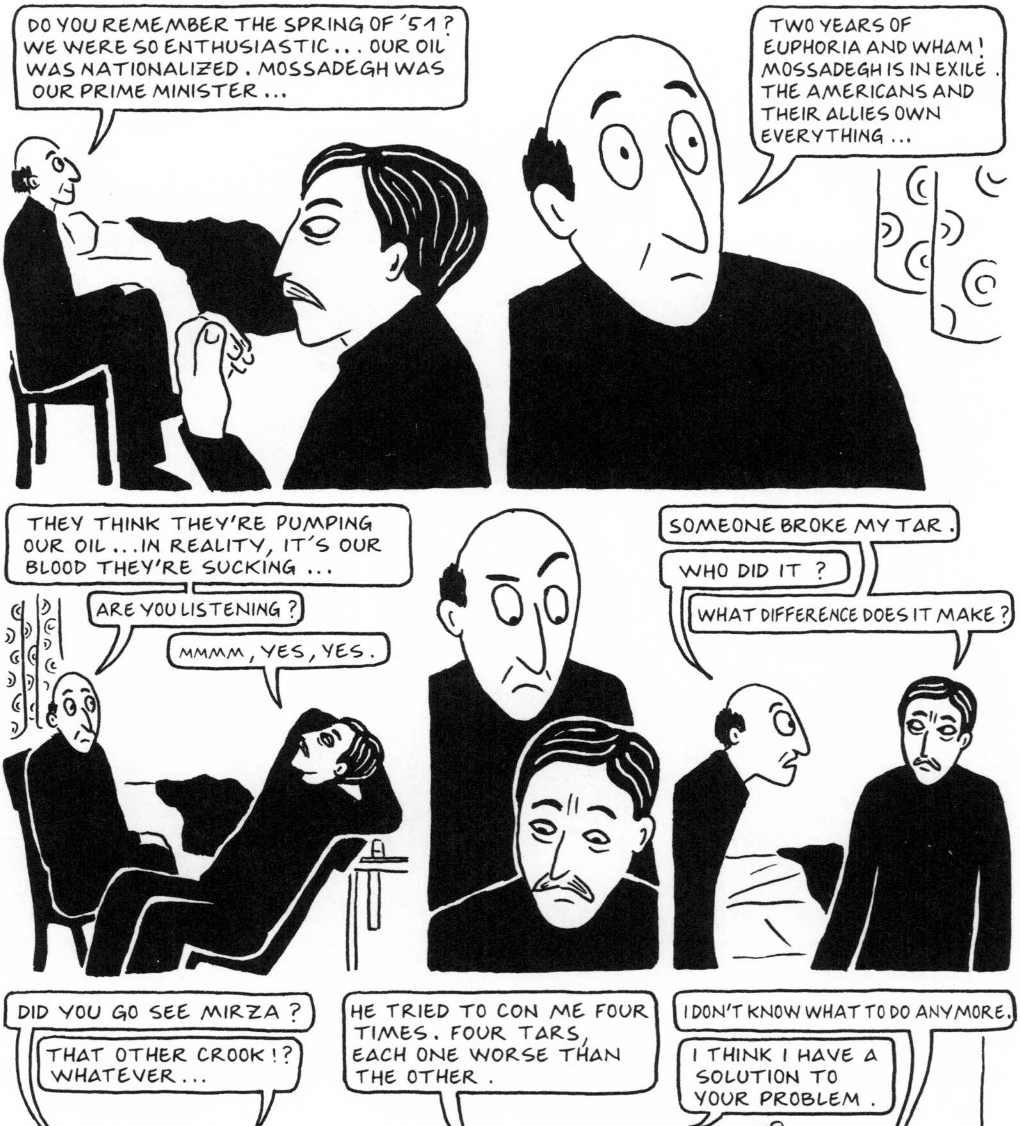
DO YOU REMEMBER THE SPRING OF '51? WE WERE SO ENTHUSIASTIC... OUR OIL WAS NATIONALIZED. MOSSADEGH WAS OUR PRIME MINISTER...
TWO YEARS OF EUPHORIA AND WHAM! MOSSADEGH IS IN EXILE. THE AMERICANS AND THEIR ALLIES OWN EVERYTHING...
THEY THINK THEY'RE PUMPING OUR OIL... IN REALITY, IT'S OUR BLOOD THEY'RE SUCKING...
ARE YOU LISTENING?
MMMM, YES, YES.
SOMEONE BROKE MY TAR.
WHO DID IT?
WHAT DIFFERENCE DOES IT MAKE?
DID YOU GO SEE MIRZA?
THAT OTHER CROOK!? WHATEVER...
HE TRIED TO CON ME FOUR TIMES. FOUR TARS, EACH ONE WORSE THAN THE OTHER.
I DON'T KNOW WHAT TO DO ANYMORE.
I THINK I HAVE A SOLUTION TO YOUR PROBLEM.

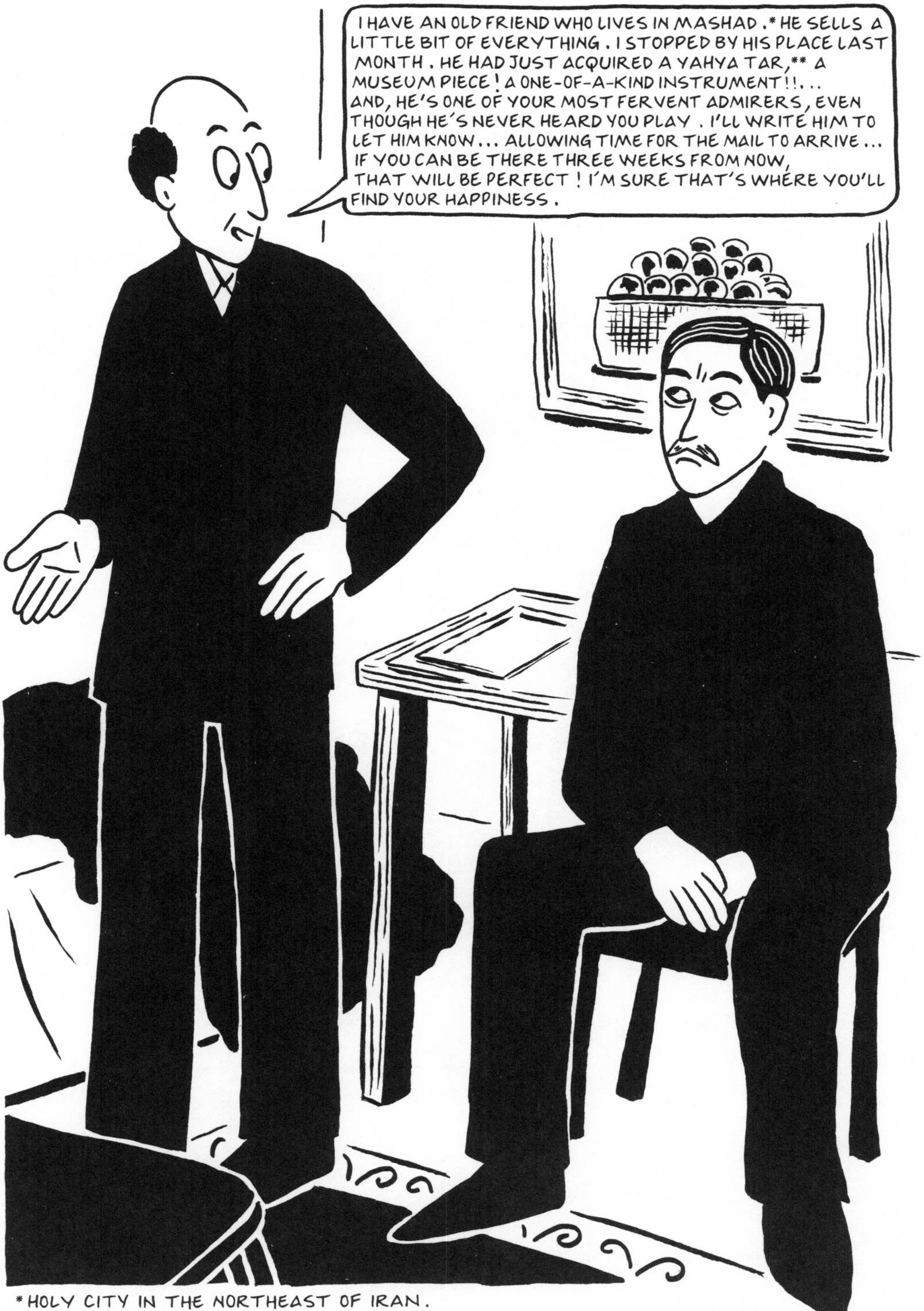
I HAVE AN OLD FRIEND WHO LIVES IN MASHAD.* HE SELLS A LITTLE BIT OF EVERYTHING. I STOPPED BY HIS PLACE LAST MONTH. HE HAD JUST ACQUIRED A YAHYA TAR,** A MUSEUM PIECE! A ONE-OF-A-KIND INSTRUMENT!!.. AND, HE'S ONE OF YOUR MOST FERVENT ADMIRERS, EVEN THOUGH HE'S NEVER HEARD YOU PLAY. I'LL WRITE HIM TO LET HIM KNOW... ALLOWING TIME FOR THE MAIL TO ARRIVE... IF YOU CAN BE THERE THREE WEEKS FROM NOW, THAT WILL BE PERFECT! I'M SURE THAT'S WHERE YOU'LL FIND YOUR HAPPINESS.

*HOLY CITY IN THE NORTHEAST OF IRAN.
**THE EQUIVALENT OF A STRADIVARIUS VIOLIN.

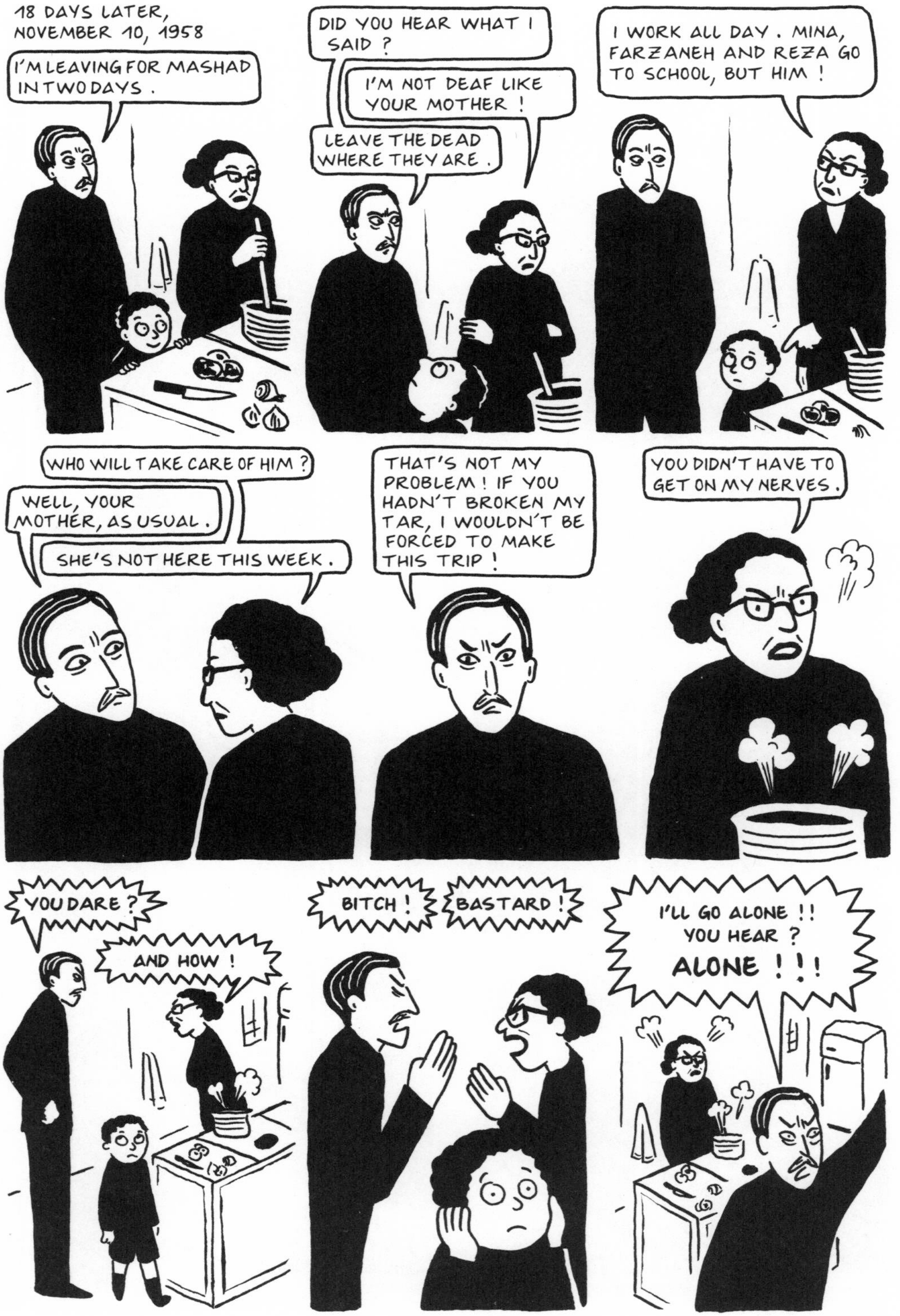
18 DAYS LATER, NOVEMBER 10, 1958
I'M LEAVING FOR MASHAD IN TWO DAYS.
DID YOU HEAR WHAT I SAID?
LEAVE THE DEAD WHERE THEY ARE.
I'M NOT DEAF LIKE YOUR MOTHER!
I WORK ALL DAY. MINA, FARZANEH AND REZA GO TO SCHOOL, BUT HIM!
WHO WILL TAKE CARE OF HIM?
WELL, YOUR MOTHER, AS USUAL.
SHE'S NOT HERE THIS WEEK.
THAT'S NOT MY PROBLEM! IF YOU HADN'T BROKEN MY TAR, I WOULDN'T BE FORCED TO MAKE THIS TRIP!
YOU DIDN'T HAVE TO GET ON MY NERVES.
YOU DARE?
AND HOW!
BITCH!
BASTARD!
I'LL GO ALONE!! YOU HEAR? ALONE!!!

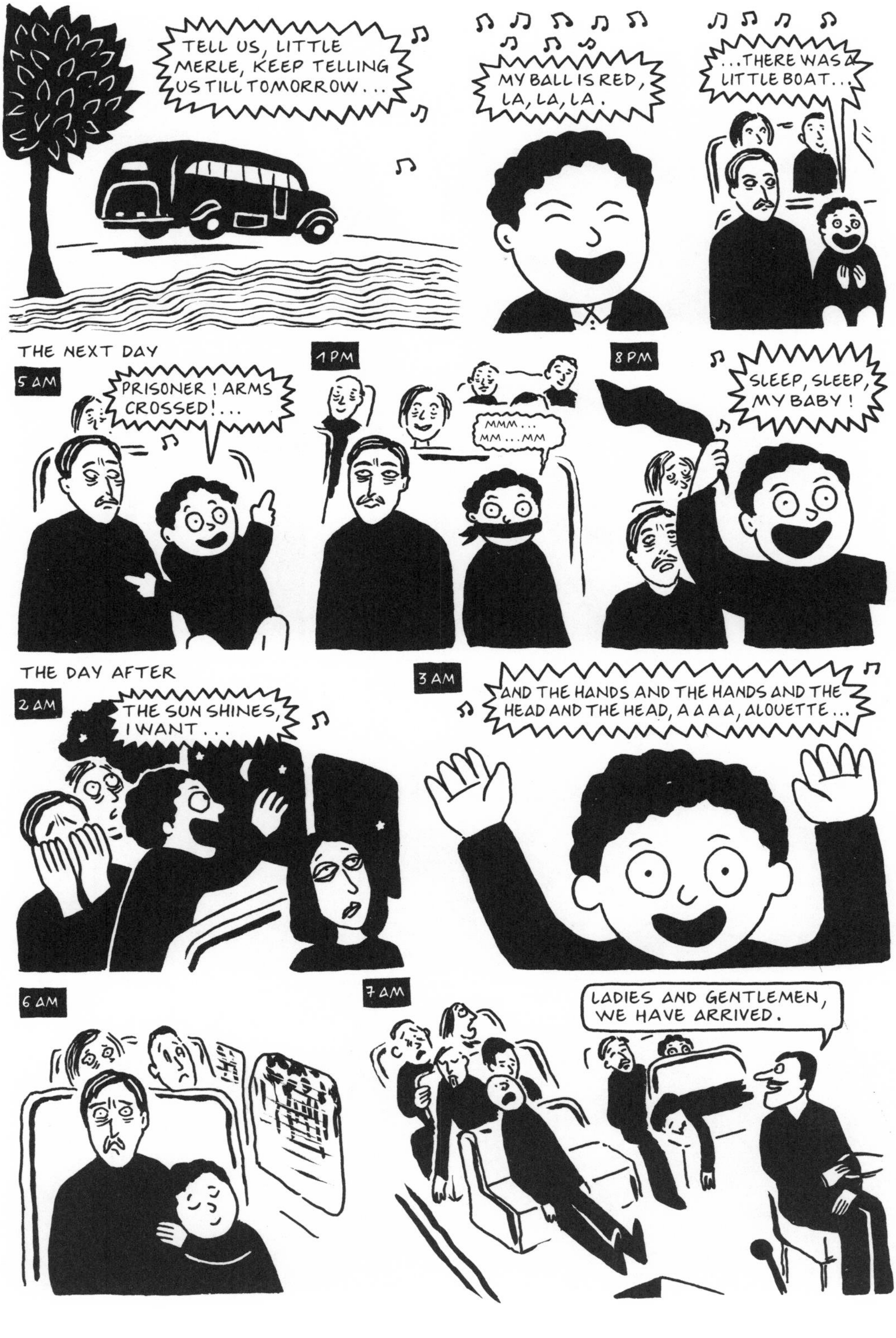
TELL US, LITTLE MERLE, KEEP TELLING US TILL TOMORROW...
MY BALL IS RED, LA, LA, LA.
...THERE WAS A LITTLE BOAT...
THE NEXT DAY
5 AM
PRISONER! ARMS CROSSED!...
1 PM
MMM... MM...MM
8 PM
SLEEP, SLEEP, MY BABY!
THE DAY AFTER
2 AM
THE SUN SHINES, I WANT...
3 AM
AND THE HANDS AND THE HANDS AND THE HEAD AND THE HEAD, A A A A, ALOUETTE...
6 AM
7 AM
LADIES AND GENTLEMEN, WE HAVE ARRIVED.

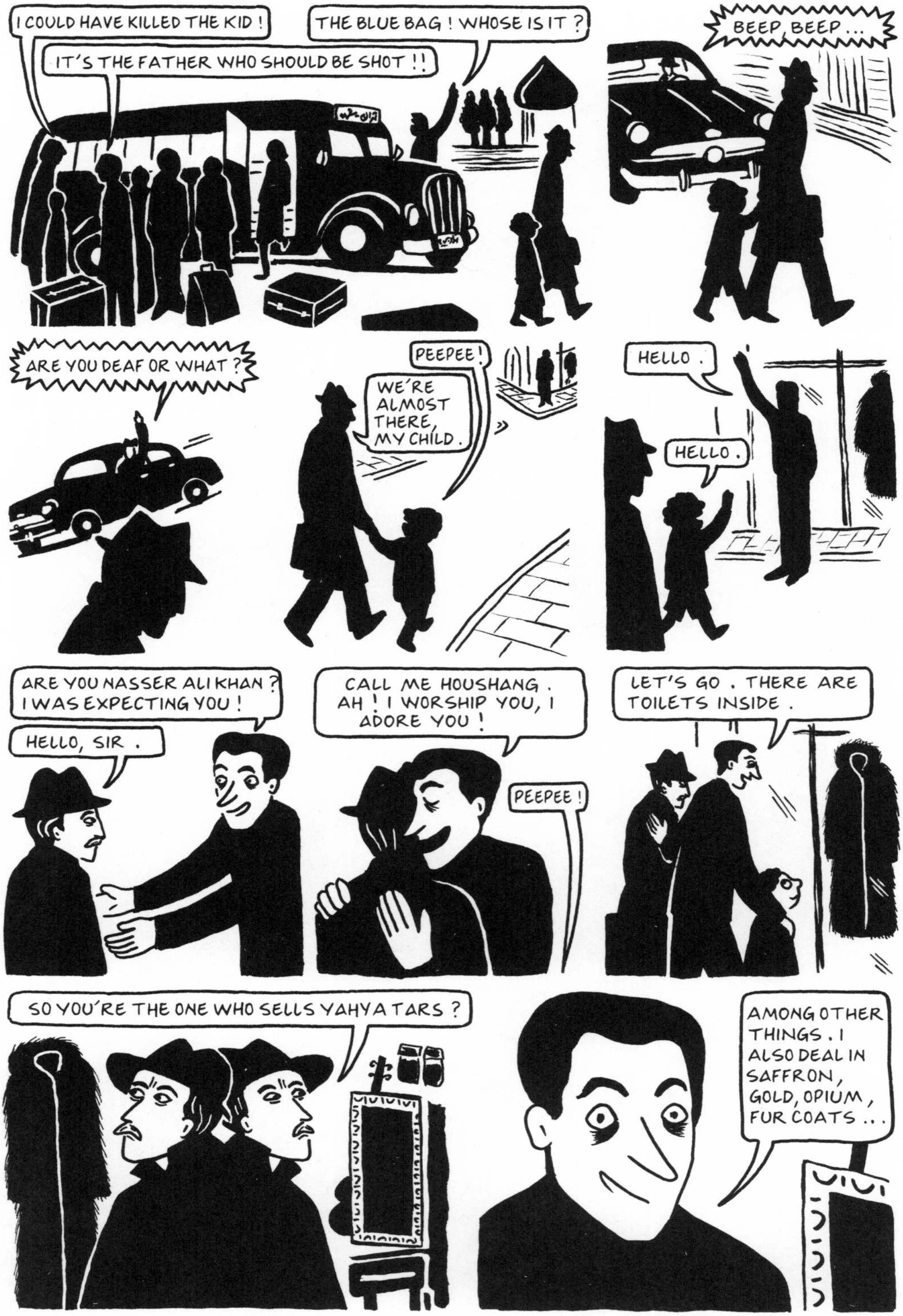
I COULD HAVE KILLED THE KID!
IT'S THE FATHER WHO SHOULD BE SHOT!!
THE BLUE BAG! WHOSE IS IT?
BEEP, BEEP...
ARE YOU DEAF OR WHAT?
PEEPEE!
WE'RE ALMOST THERE, MY CHILD.
HELLO.
HELLO.
ARE YOU NASSER ALI KHAN? I WAS EXPECTING YOU!
HELLO, SIR.
CALL ME HOUSHANG. AH! I WORSHIP YOU, I ADORE YOU!
PEEPEE!
LET'S GO. THERE ARE TOILETS INSIDE.
SO YOU'RE THE ONE WHO SELLS YAHYA TARS?
AMONG OTHER THINGS. I ALSO DEAL IN SAFFRON, GOLD, OPIUM, FUR COATS...

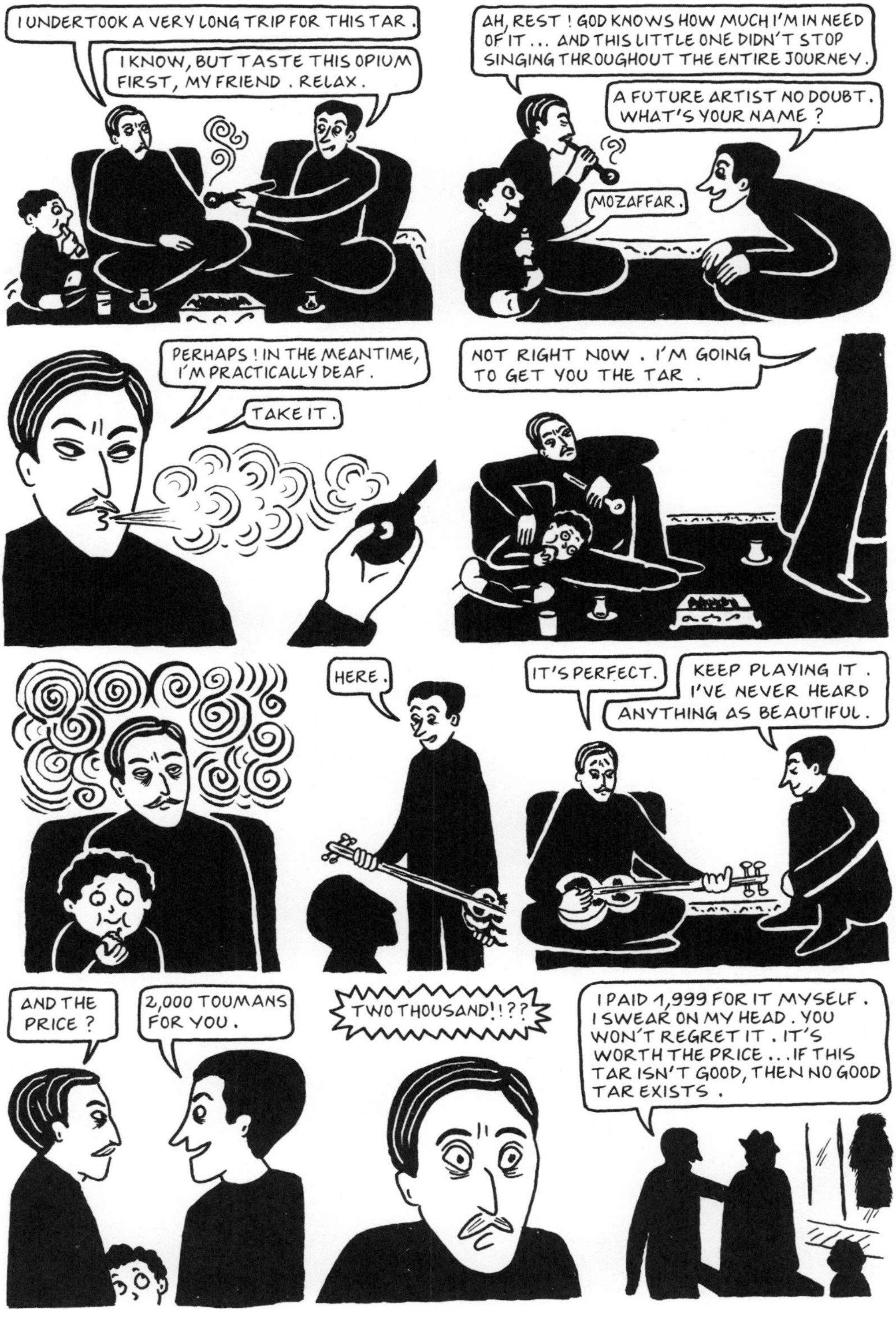
I UNDERTOOK A VERY LONG TRIP FOR THIS TAR.
I KNOW, BUT TASTE THIS OPIUM FIRST, MY FRIEND. RELAX.
AH, REST! GOD KNOWS HOW MUCH I'M IN NEED OF IT... AND THIS LITTLE ONE DIDN'T STOP SINGING THROUGHOUT THE ENTIRE JOURNEY.
A FUTURE ARTIST NO DOUBT. WHAT'S YOUR NAME?
MOZAFFAR.
PERHAPS! IN THE MEANTIME, I'M PRACTICALLY DEAF.
TAKE IT.
NOT RIGHT NOW. I'M GOING TO GET YOU THE TAR.
HERE.
IT'S PERFECT.
KEEP PLAYING IT. I'VE NEVER HEARD ANYTHING AS BEAUTIFUL.
AND THE PRICE?
2,000 TOUMANS FOR YOU.
TWO THOUSAND!!??
I PAID 1,999 FOR IT MYSELF. I SWEAR ON MY HEAD. YOU WON'T REGRET IT. IT'S WORTH THE PRICE... IF THIS TAR ISN'T GOOD, THEN NO GOOD TAR EXISTS.

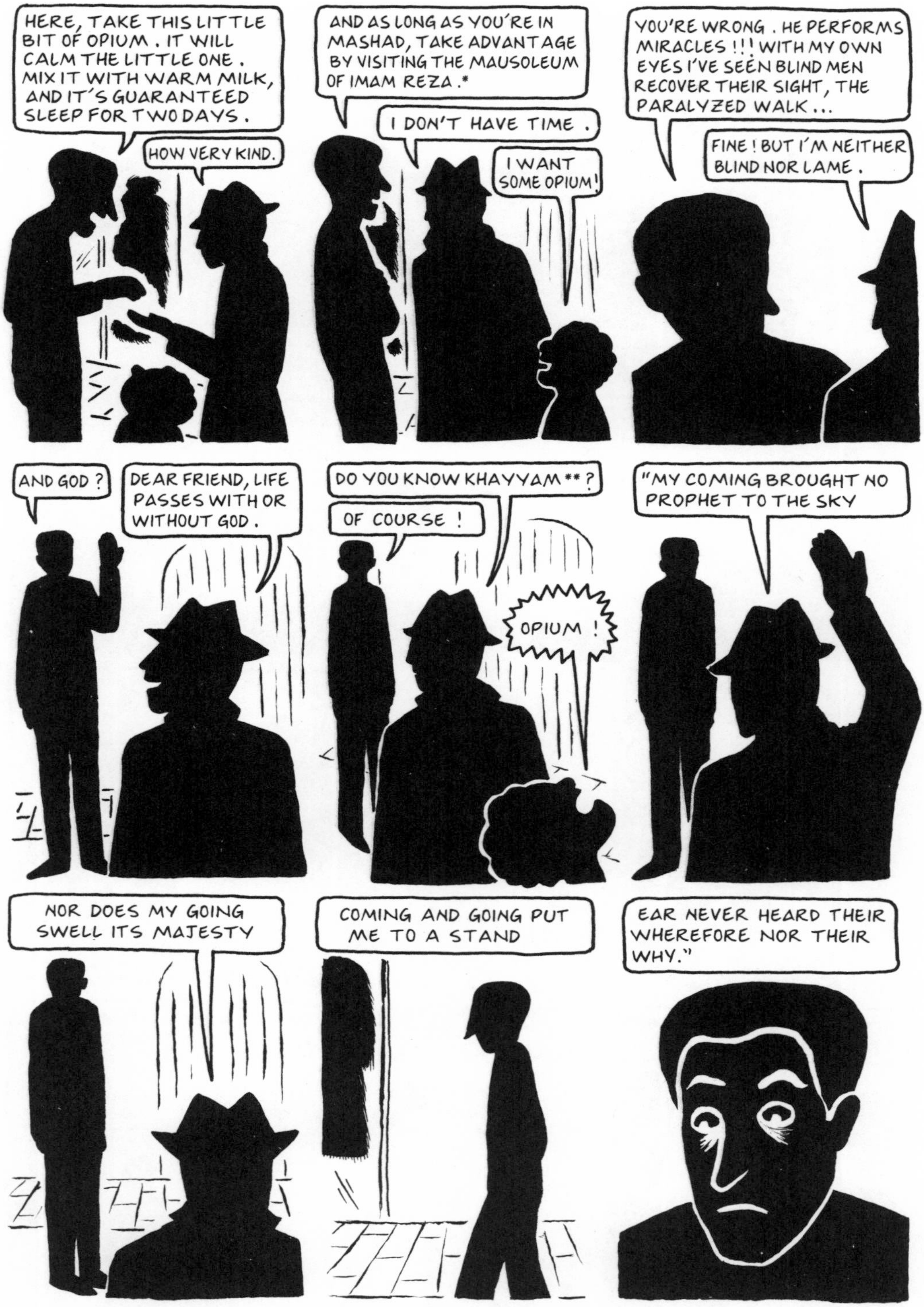
HERE, TAKE THIS LITTLE BIT OF OPIUM. IT WILL CALM THE LITTLE ONE. MIX IT WITH WARM MILK, AND IT'S GUARANTEED SLEEP FOR TWO DAYS.
HOW VERY KIND.
AND AS LONG AS YOU'RE IN MASHAD, TAKE ADVANTAGE BY VISITING THE MAUSOLEUM OF IMAM REZA.*
I DON'T HAVE TIME.
I WANT SOME OPIUM!
YOU'RE WRONG. HE PERFORMS MIRACLES!!! WITH MY OWN EYES I'VE SEEN BLIND MEN RECOVER THEIR SIGHT, THE PARALYZED WALK...
FINE! BUT I'M NEITHER BLIND NOR LAME.
AND GOD?
DEAR FRIEND, LIFE PASSES WITH OR WITHOUT GOD.
DO YOU KNOW KHAYYAM**?
OF COURSE!
OPIUM!
"MY COMING BROUGHT NO PROPHET TO THE SKY
NOR DOES MY GOING SWELL ITS MAJESTY
COMING AND GOING PUT ME TO A STAND
EAR NEVER HEARD THEIR WHEREFORE NOR THEIR WHY."

*EIGHTH IMAM OF THE SHIITES. **IRANIAN POET (1048-1131).

THEY LEFT THAT VERY NIGHT...

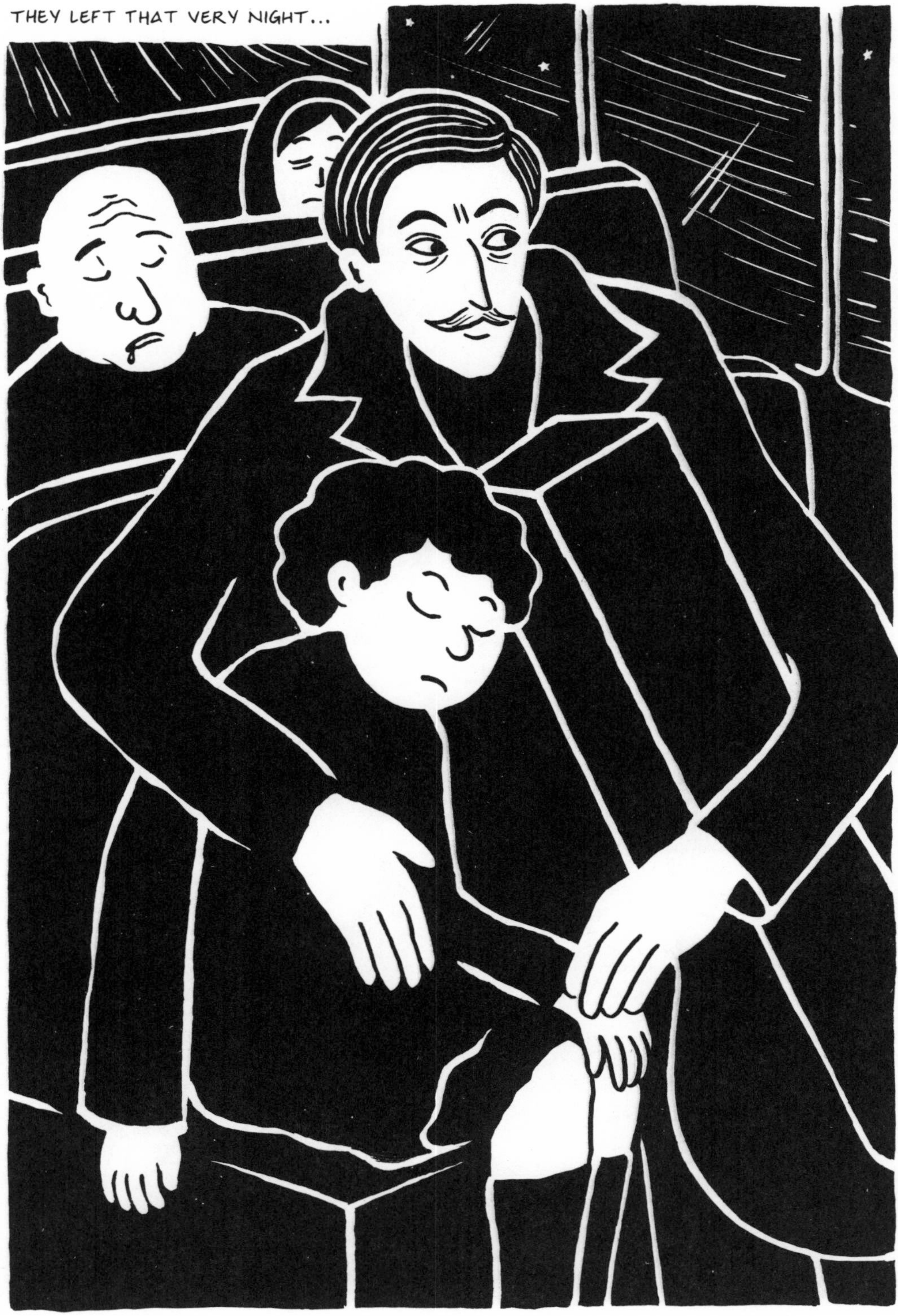

...AND ARRIVED TWO NIGHTS LATER IN TEHRAN. NASSER ALI KHAN PUT MOZAFFAR TO BED. HE HAD ONLY ONE DESIRE: TO PLAY HIS TAR. BUT HE TOLD HIMSELF HE SHOULD WAIT UNTIL MORNING.

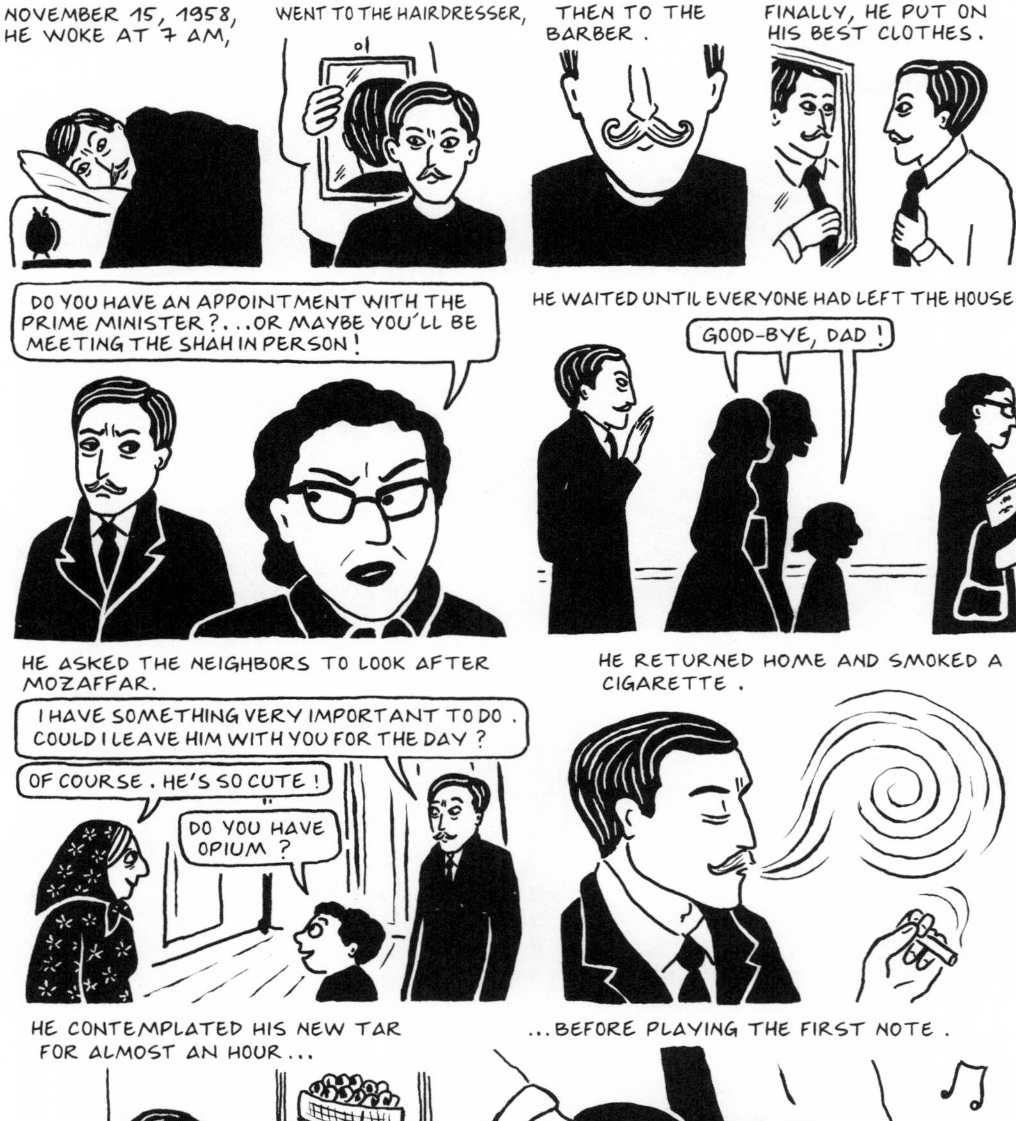
NOVEMBER 15, 1958, HE WOKE AT 7 AM,
WENT TO THE HAIRDRESSER,
THEN TO THE BARBER.
FINALLY, HE PUT ON HIS BEST CLOTHES.
DO YOU HAVE AN APPOINTMENT WITH THE PRIME MINISTER?...OR MAYBE YOU'LL BE MEETING THE SHAH IN PERSON!
HE WAITED UNTIL EVERYONE HAD LEFT THE HOUSE.
GOOD-BYE, DAD!
HE ASKED THE NEIGHBORS TO LOOK AFTER MOZAFFAR.
I HAVE SOMETHING VERY IMPORTANT TO DO. COULD I LEAVE HIM WITH YOU FOR THE DAY?
OF COURSE. HE'S SO CUTE!
DO YOU HAVE OPIUM?
HE RETURNED HOME AND SMOKED A CIGARETTE.
HE CONTEMPLATED HIS NEW TAR FOR ALMOST AN HOUR...
...BEFORE PLAYING THE FIRST NOTE.

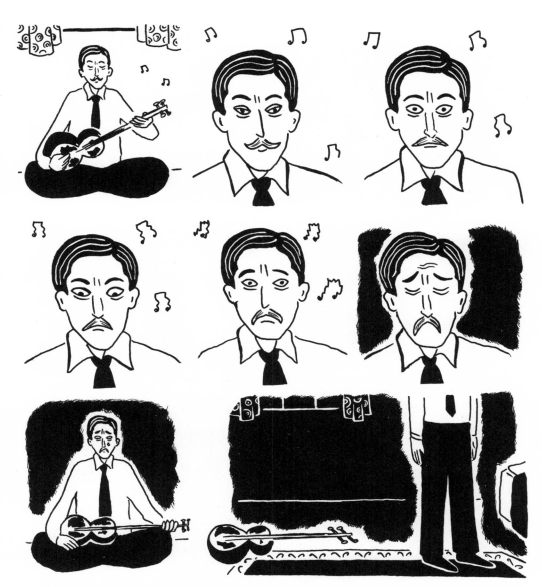

SINCE NO OTHER TAR COULD GIVE HIM THE PLEASURE OF PLAYING, NASSER ALI KHAN DECIDED TO DIE . HE LAY DOWN IN HIS BED ...

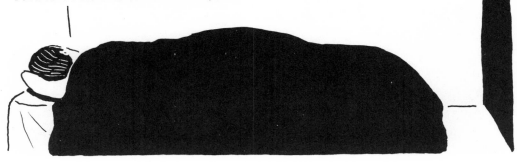

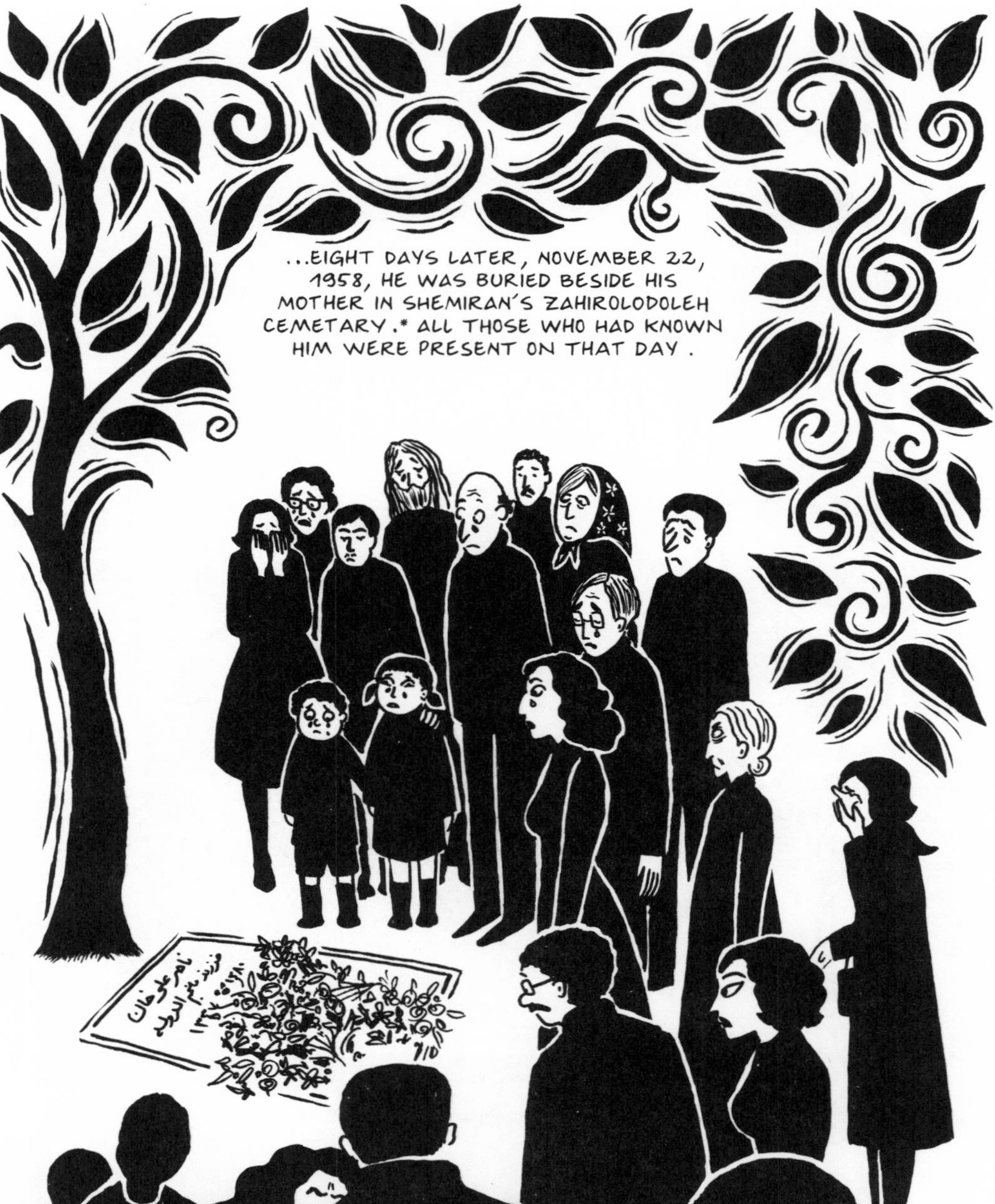
...EIGHT DAYS LATER, NOVEMBER 22, 1958, HE WAS BURIED BESIDE HIS MOTHER IN SHEMIRAN'S ZAHIROLODOLEH CEMETARY.* ALL THOSE WHO HAD KNOWN HIM WERE PRESENT ON THAT DAY.

* LOCATED NORTH OF TEHRAN.

THE FIRST DAY

NOVEMBER 15, 1958

NOVEMBER 15, 1958 . NASSER ALI KHAN MADE UP HIS MIND TO SURRENDER HIS SOUL . HE CONSIDERED THE DIFFERENT WAYS TO PUT AN END TO HIS DAYS .

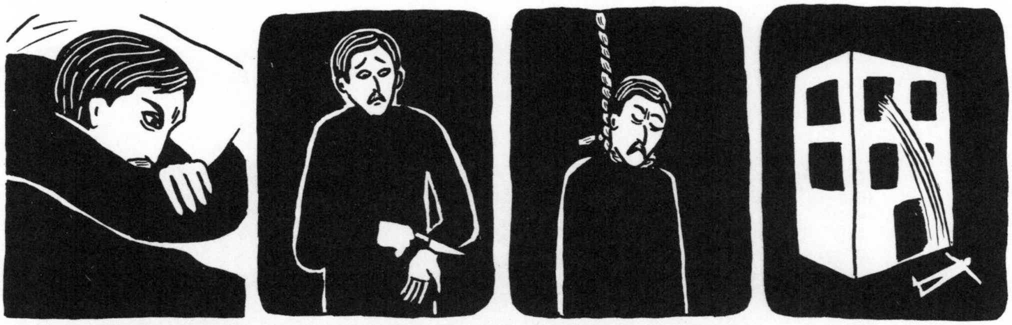

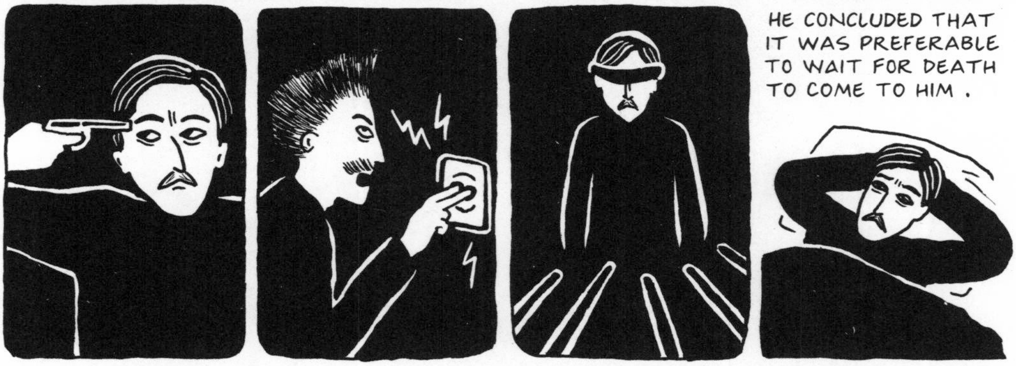
HE CONCLUDED THAT IT WAS PREFERABLE TO WAIT FOR DEATH TO COME TO HIM .

THE SAME DAY AT FOUR O'CLOCK, HIS WIFE, NAHID, A TEACHER BY PROFESSION, RETURNED FROM SCHOOL WITH HER FIRST THREE CHILDREN, MINA, REZA AND FARZANEH .

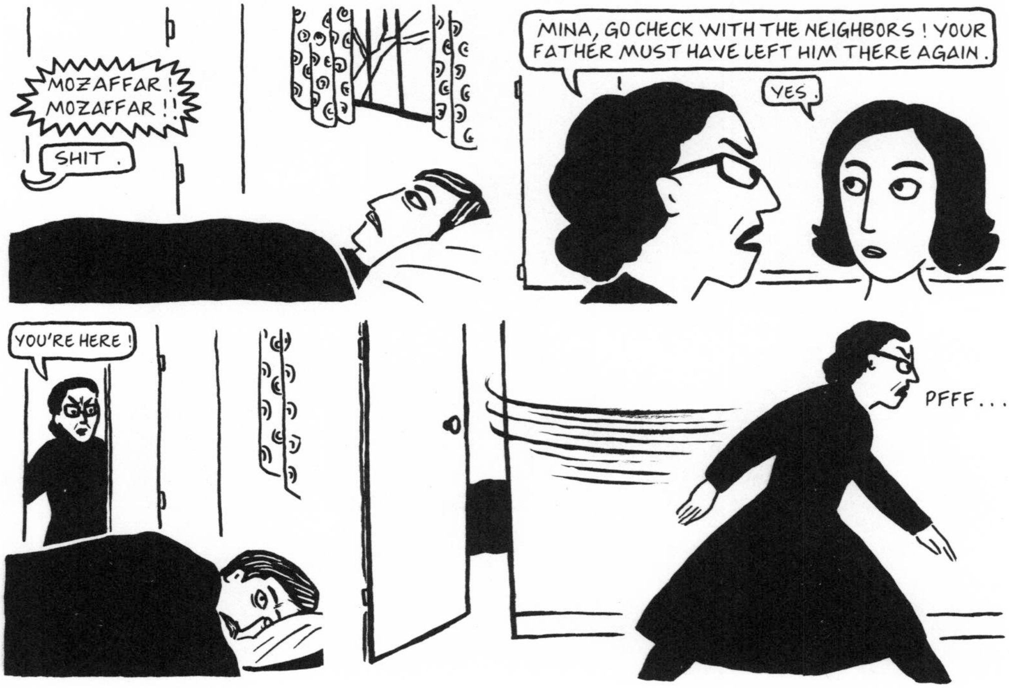
MOZAFFAR ! MOZAFFAR ! !
SHIT .
MINA, GO CHECK WITH THE NEIGHBORS ! YOUR FATHER MUST HAVE LEFT HIM THERE AGAIN .
YES .
YOU'RE HERE !
PFFF . . .

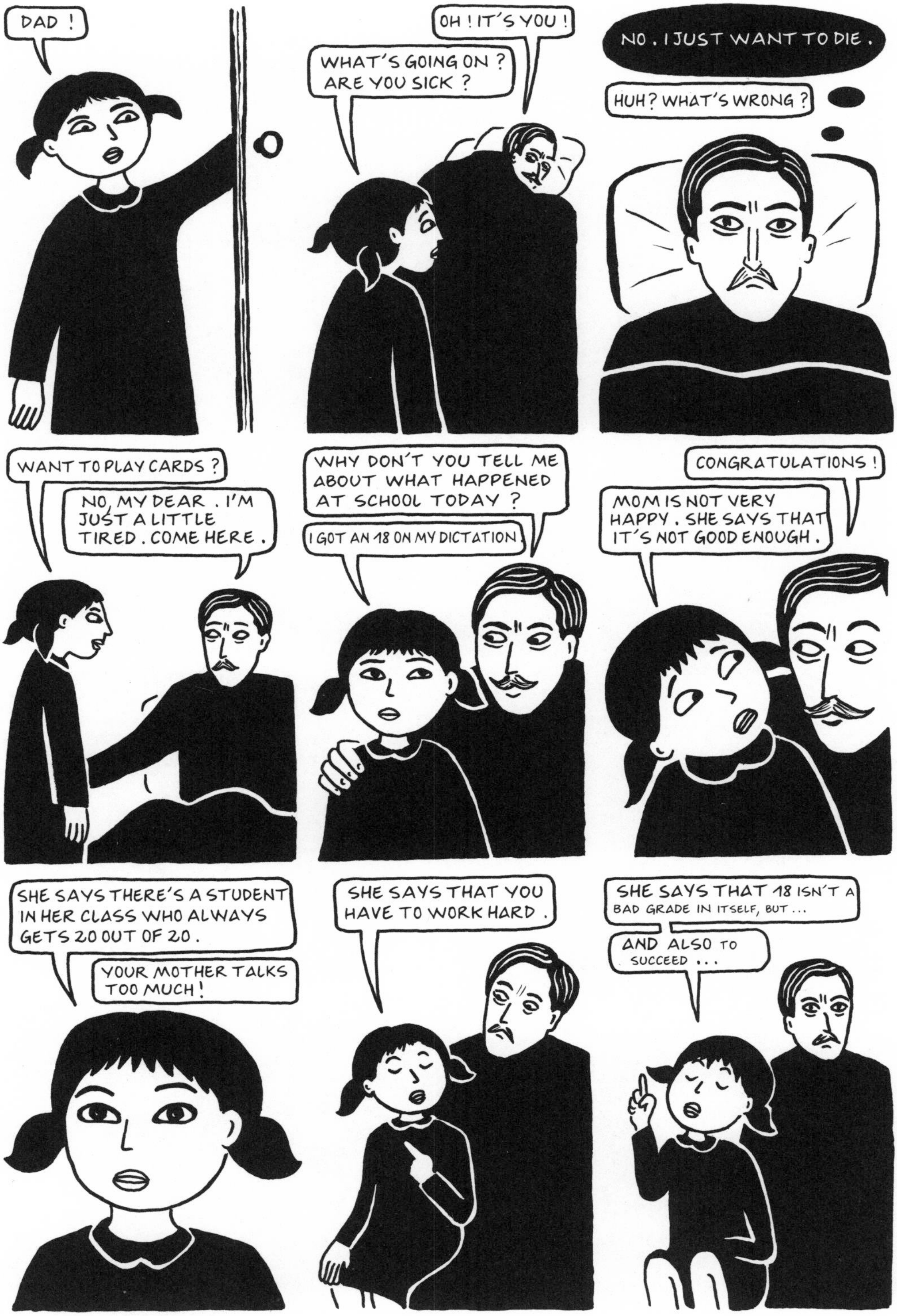
DAD !
OH ! IT'S YOU !
WHAT'S GOING ON ? ARE YOU SICK ?
NO. I JUST WANT TO DIE.
HUH ? WHAT'S WRONG ?
WANT TO PLAY CARDS ?
NO, MY DEAR. I'M JUST A LITTLE TIRED. COME HERE.
WHY DON'T YOU TELL ME ABOUT WHAT HAPPENED AT SCHOOL TODAY ?
I GOT AN 18 ON MY DICTATION.
CONGRATULATIONS !
MOM IS NOT VERY HAPPY. SHE SAYS THAT IT'S NOT GOOD ENOUGH.
SHE SAYS THERE'S A STUDENT IN HER CLASS WHO ALWAYS GETS 20 OUT OF 20.
YOUR MOTHER TALKS TOO MUCH !
SHE SAYS THAT YOU HAVE TO WORK HARD.
SHE SAYS THAT 18 ISN'T A BAD GRADE IN ITSELF, BUT ...
AND ALSO TO SUCCEED ...

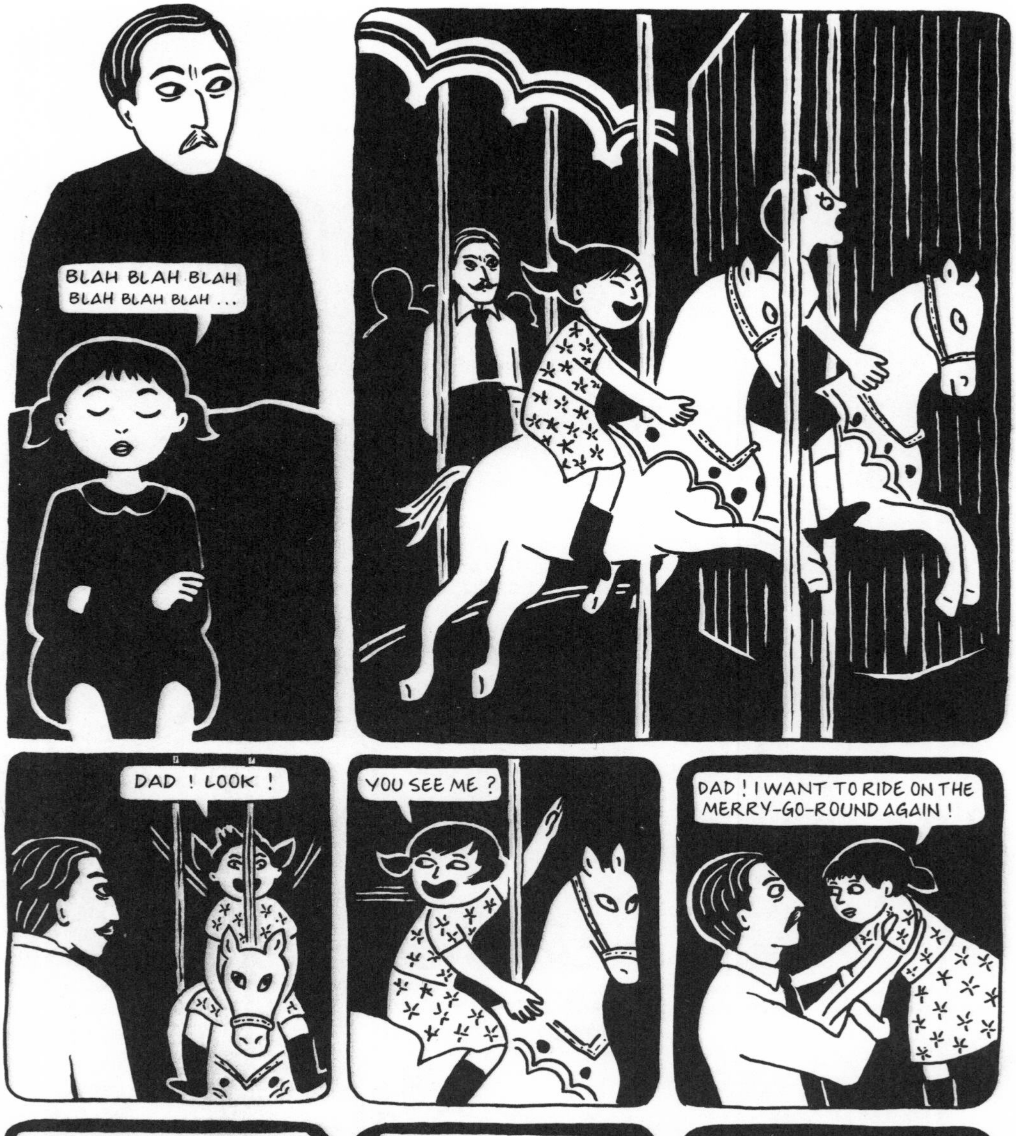
BLAH BLAH BLAH
BLAH BLAH BLAH ...
DAD ! LOOK !
YOU SEE ME ?
DAD ! I WANT TO RIDE ON THE MERRY-GO-ROUND AGAIN !
YOU'VE ALREADY GONE TWICE !
BUT, DAD ...
COME, WE'RE GOING TO GO SEE SOMETHING ELSE.
WHERE'S MY RABBIT ?
I ATE IT !
WILL YOU BUY ME ONE OF THOSE TALKING DOLLS ?
BUT, MY DEAR, THEY DON'T TALK.

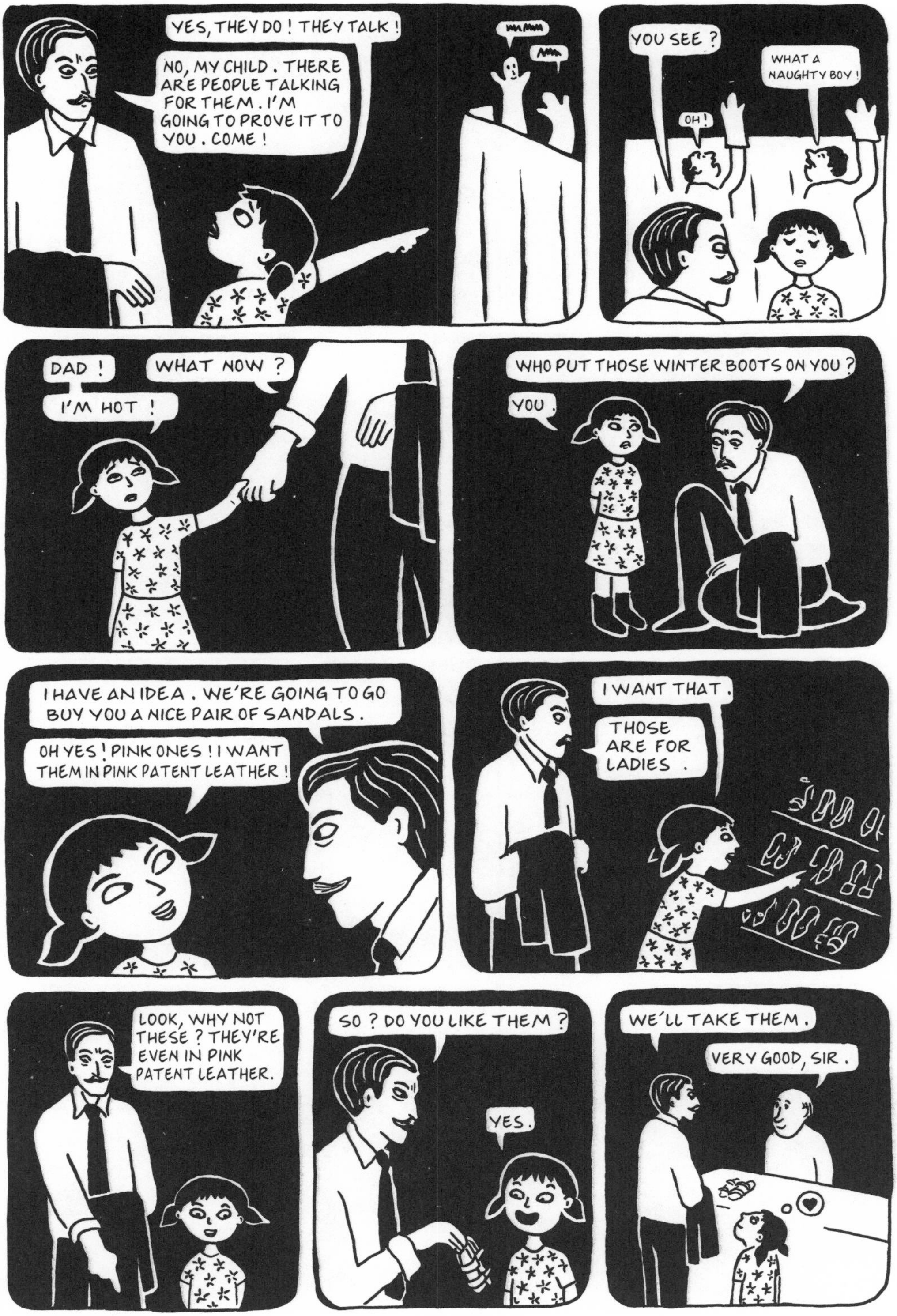

YES, THEY DO! THEY TALK!
NO, MY CHILD. THERE ARE PEOPLE TALKING FOR THEM. I'M GOING TO PROVE IT TO YOU. COME!
YOU SEE?
OH!
WHAT A NAUGHTY BOY!
DAD!
I'M HOT!
WHAT NOW?
WHO PUT THOSE WINTER BOOTS ON YOU?
YOU.
I HAVE AN IDEA. WE'RE GOING TO GO BUY YOU A NICE PAIR OF SANDALS.
OH YES! PINK ONES! I WANT THEM IN PINK PATENT LEATHER!
I WANT THAT.
THOSE ARE FOR LADIES.
LOOK, WHY NOT THESE? THEY'RE EVEN IN PINK PATENT LEATHER.
SO? DO YOU LIKE THEM?
YES.
WE'LL TAKE THEM.
VERY GOOD, SIR.

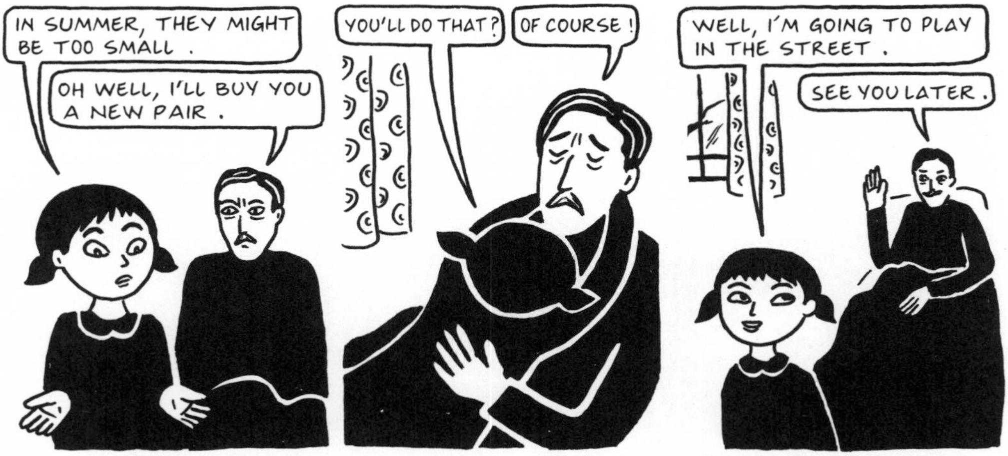
IN SUMMER, THEY MIGHT BE TOO SMALL .
OH WELL, I'LL BUY YOU A NEW PAIR .
YOU'LL DO THAT ?
OF COURSE !
WELL, I'M GOING TO PLAY IN THE STREET .
SEE YOU LATER .

OF HIS FOUR CHILDREN, FARZANEH WAS HER FATHER'S FAVORITE . POSSESSED BY AN UNUSUAL INTEREST IN MORPHOPSYCHOLOGY, NASSER ALI KHAN WAS CONVINCED THAT HIS PHYSICAL RESEMBLANCE TO HIS YOUNGEST DAUGHTER PROVED THE CLOSENESS OF THEIR SOULS . AND HE WASN'T WRONG . THEY WERE BOTH VERY INTELLIGENT, LIVELY AND SPIRITUAL BEINGS . I REMEMBER IN 1998, DURING ONE OF MY VISITS TO TEHRAN...

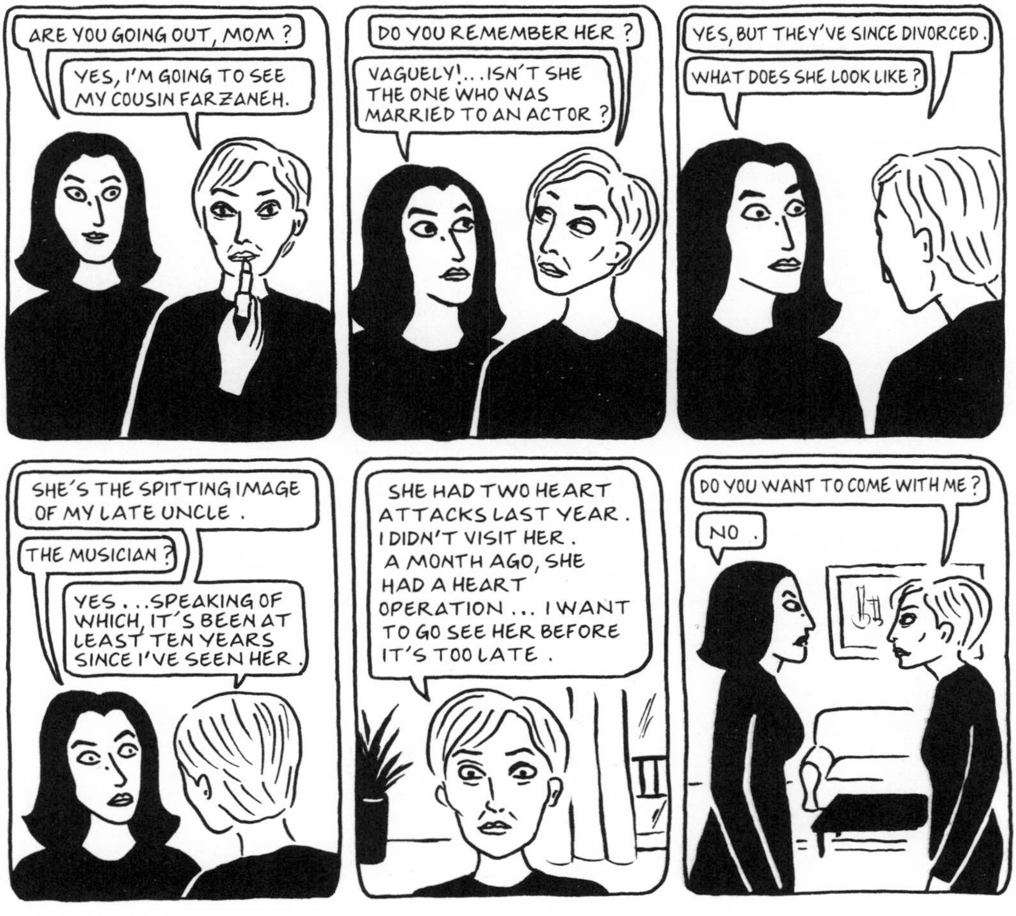
ARE YOU GOING OUT, MOM ?
YES, I'M GOING TO SEE MY COUSIN FARZANEH.
DO YOU REMEMBER HER ?
VAGUELY! . . . ISN'T SHE THE ONE WHO WAS MARRIED TO AN ACTOR ?
YES, BUT THEY'VE SINCE DIVORCED .
WHAT DOES SHE LOOK LIKE ?
SHE'S THE SPITTING IMAGE OF MY LATE UNCLE .
THE MUSICIAN ?
YES . . . SPEAKING OF WHICH, IT'S BEEN AT LEAST TEN YEARS SINCE I'VE SEEN HER .
SHE HAD TWO HEART ATTACKS LAST YEAR . I DIDN'T VISIT HER . A MONTH AGO, SHE HAD A HEART OPERATION . . . I WANT TO GO SEE HER BEFORE IT'S TOO LATE .
DO YOU WANT TO COME WITH ME ?
NO .

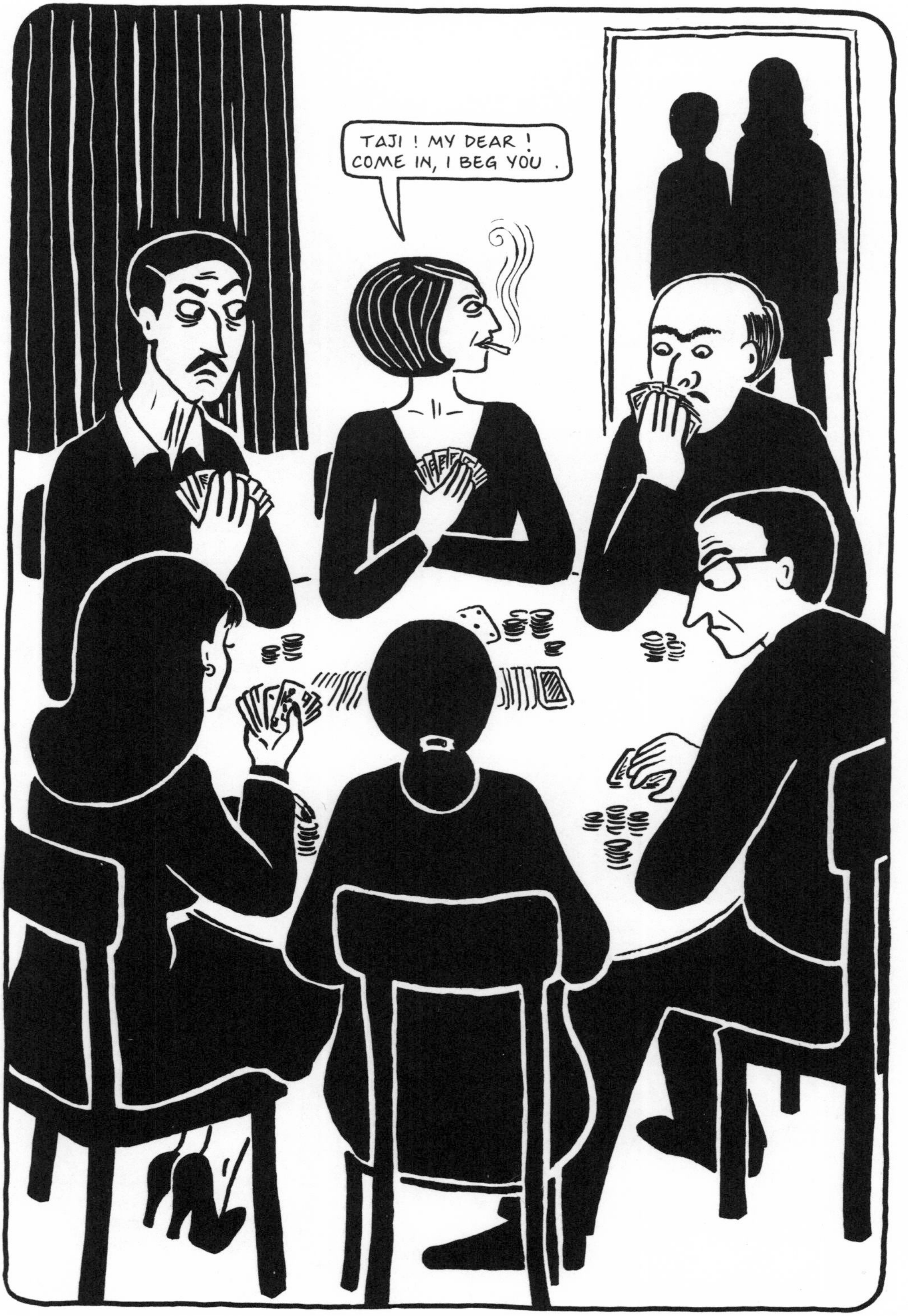
TAJI ! MY DEAR ! COME IN, I BEG YOU .

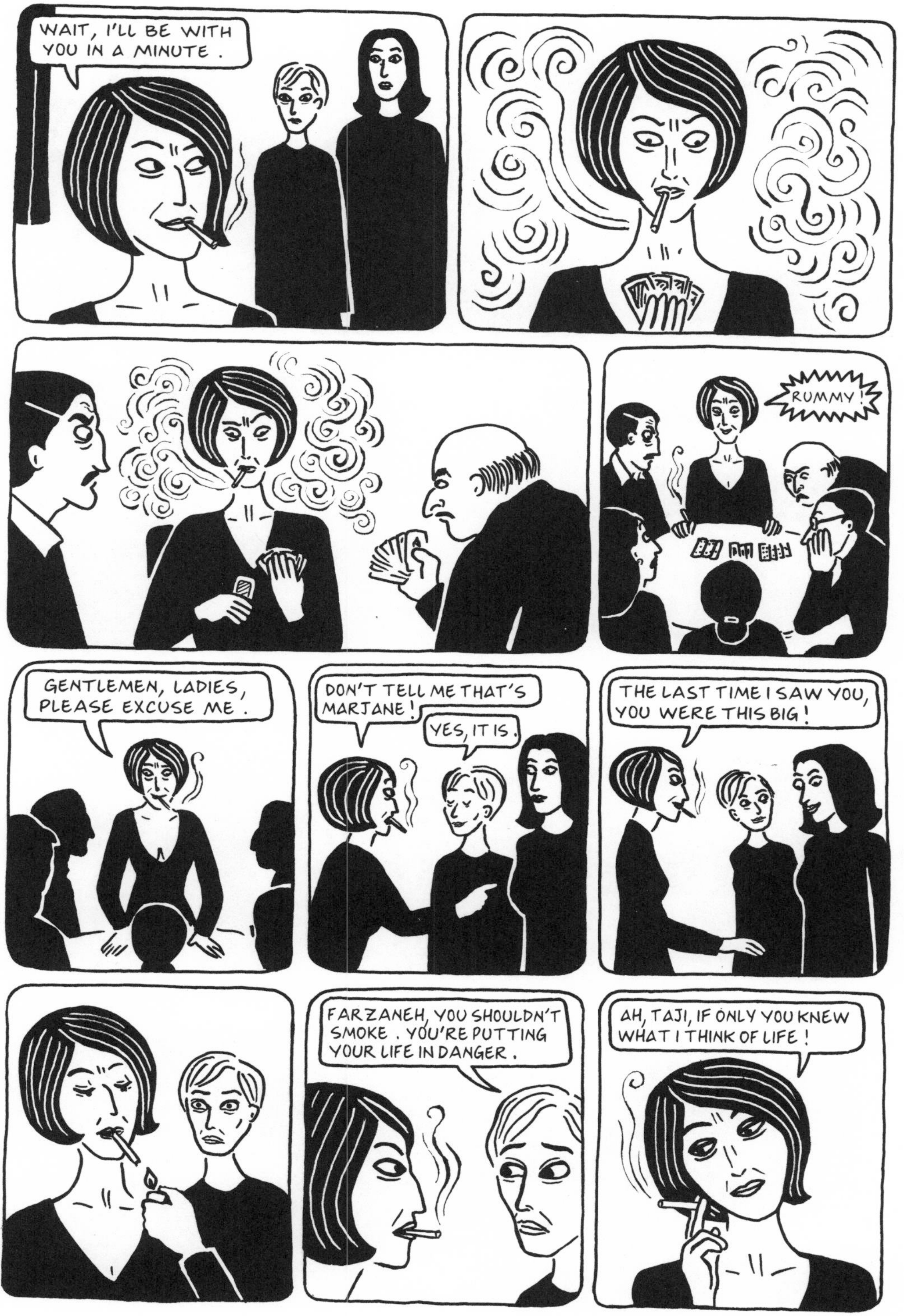
WAIT, I'LL BE WITH YOU IN A MINUTE.
RUMMY!
GENTLEMEN, LADIES, PLEASE EXCUSE ME.
DON'T TELL ME THAT'S MARJANE!
YES, IT IS.
THE LAST TIME I SAW YOU, YOU WERE THIS BIG!
FARZANEH, YOU SHOULDN'T SMOKE. YOU'RE PUTTING YOUR LIFE IN DANGER.
AH, TAJI, IF ONLY YOU KNEW WHAT I THINK OF LIFE!

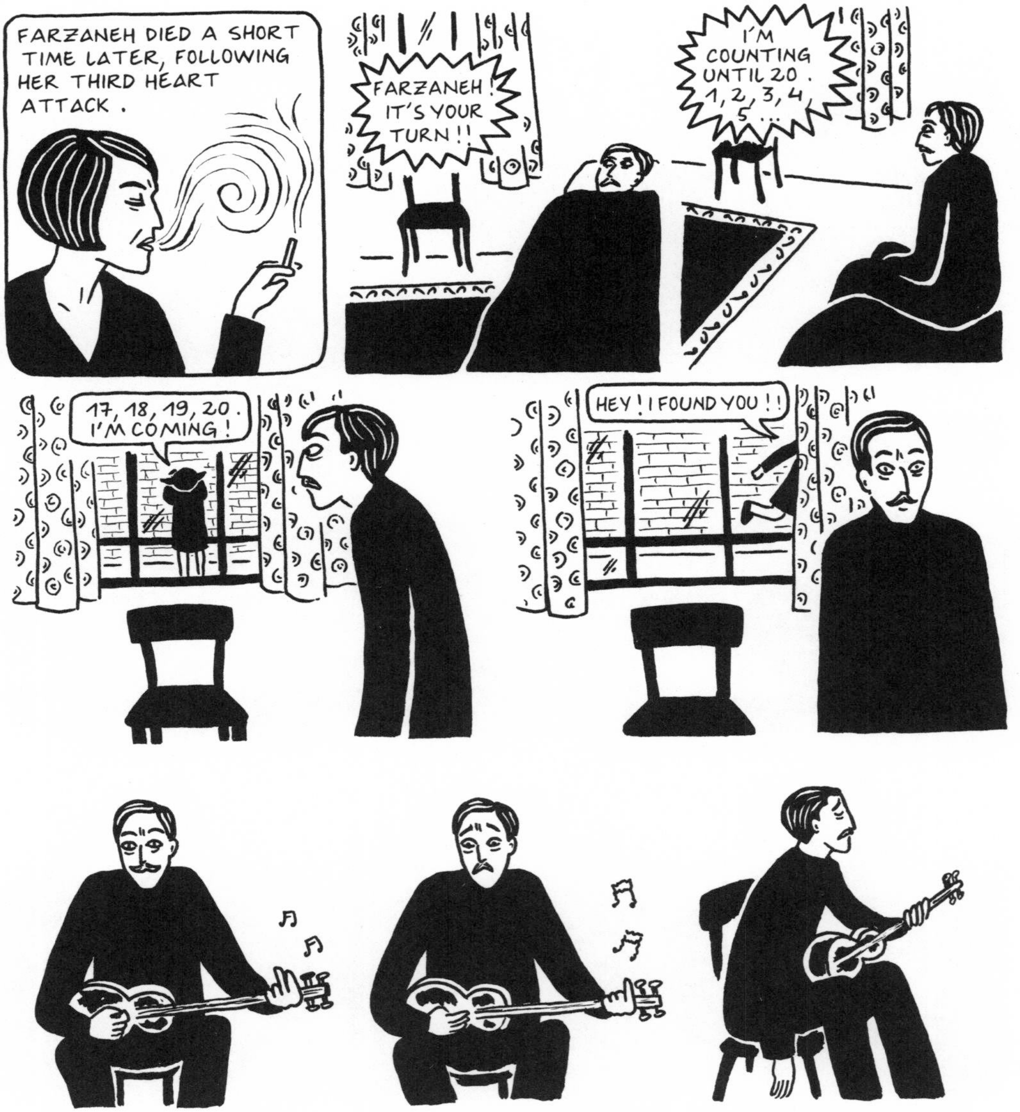
FARZANEH DIED A SHORT TIME LATER, FOLLOWING HER THIRD HEART ATTACK.
FARZANEH! IT'S YOUR TURN!!
I'M COUNTING UNTIL 20. 1, 2, 3, 4, 5...
17, 18, 19, 20. I'M COMING!
HEY! I FOUND YOU!!
THIS IS HOW NASSER ALI KHAN'S FIRST DAY DREW TO A CLOSE...

THE SECOND DAY

NOVEMBER 16, 1958

THE SECOND DAY FELL ON A FRIDAY. AT 12:30, NASSER ALI KHAN'S WIFE, NAHID, REALIZED THAT HER HUSBAND STILL HADN'T EMERGED FROM THE BEDROOM. SHE WAS WORRIED, BUT GIVEN THE DAMAGED STATE OF THEIR RELATIONSHIP, SHE DECIDED THAT SHE'D BE BETTER OFF CONSULTING ABDI, HER HUSBAND'S BROTHER.

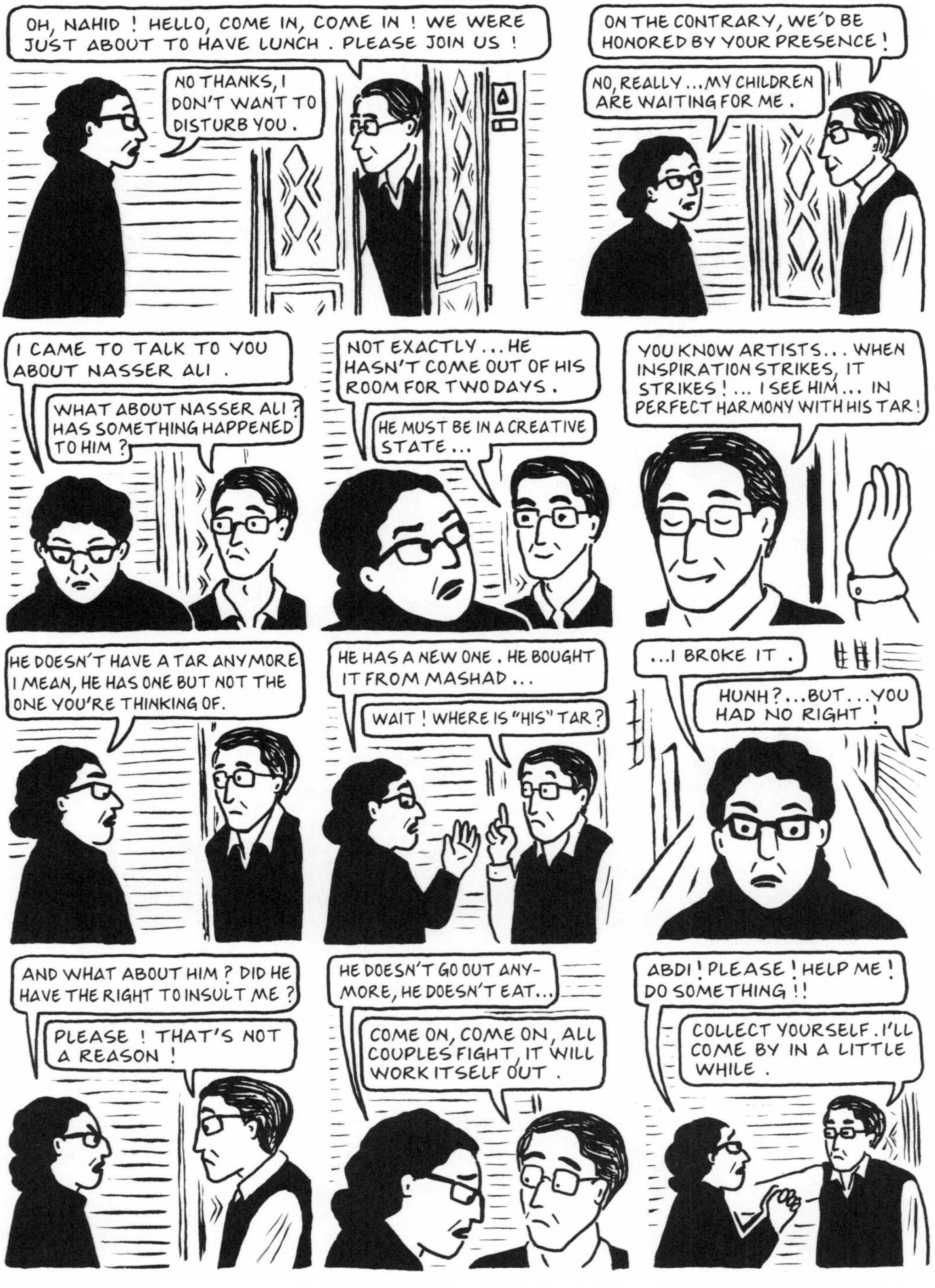
OH, NAHID! HELLO, COME IN, COME IN! WE WERE JUST ABOUT TO HAVE LUNCH. PLEASE JOIN US!
NO THANKS, I DON'T WANT TO DISTURB YOU.
ON THE CONTRARY, WE'D BE HONORED BY YOUR PRESENCE!
NO, REALLY... MY CHILDREN ARE WAITING FOR ME.
I CAME TO TALK TO YOU ABOUT NASSER ALI.
WHAT ABOUT NASSER ALI? HAS SOMETHING HAPPENED TO HIM?
NOT EXACTLY... HE HASN'T COME OUT OF HIS ROOM FOR TWO DAYS.
HE MUST BE IN A CREATIVE STATE...
YOU KNOW ARTISTS... WHEN INSPIRATION STRIKES, IT STRIKES! ... I SEE HIM... IN PERFECT HARMONY WITH HIS TAR!
HE DOESN'T HAVE A TAR ANYMORE. I MEAN, HE HAS ONE BUT NOT THE ONE YOU'RE THINKING OF.
HE HAS A NEW ONE. HE BOUGHT IT FROM MASHAD...
WAIT! WHERE IS "HIS" TAR?
...I BROKE IT.
HUNH?...BUT...YOU HAD NO RIGHT!
AND WHAT ABOUT HIM? DID HE HAVE THE RIGHT TO INSULT ME?
PLEASE! THAT'S NOT A REASON!
HE DOESN'T GO OUT ANYMORE, HE DOESN'T EAT...
COME ON, COME ON, ALL COUPLES FIGHT, IT WILL WORK ITSELF OUT.
ABDI! PLEASE! HELP ME! DO SOMETHING!!
COLLECT YOURSELF. I'LL COME BY IN A LITTLE WHILE.

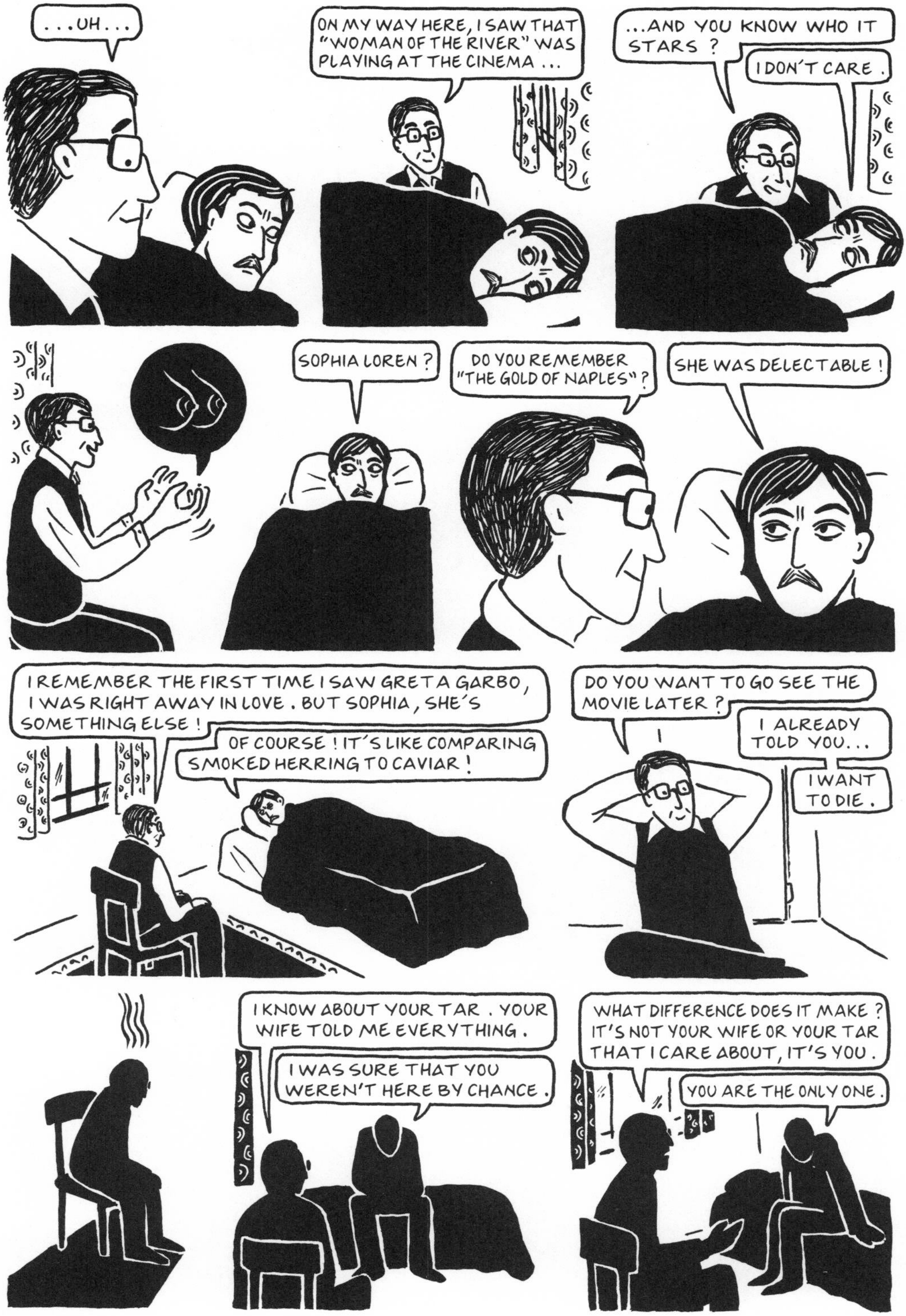
...UH...
ON MY WAY HERE, I SAW THAT "WOMAN OF THE RIVER" WAS PLAYING AT THE CINEMA...
...AND YOU KNOW WHO IT STARS?
I DON'T CARE.
SOPHIA LOREN?
DO YOU REMEMBER "THE GOLD OF NAPLES"?
SHE WAS DELECTABLE!
I REMEMBER THE FIRST TIME I SAW GRETA GARBO, I WAS RIGHT AWAY IN LOVE. BUT SOPHIA, SHE'S SOMETHING ELSE!
OF COURSE! IT'S LIKE COMPARING SMOKED HERRING TO CAVIAR!
DO YOU WANT TO GO SEE THE MOVIE LATER?
I ALREADY TOLD YOU...
I WANT TO DIE.
I KNOW ABOUT YOUR TAR. YOUR WIFE TOLD ME EVERYTHING.
I WAS SURE THAT YOU WEREN'T HERE BY CHANCE.
WHAT DIFFERENCE DOES IT MAKE? IT'S NOT YOUR WIFE OR YOUR TAR THAT I CARE ABOUT, IT'S YOU.
YOU ARE THE ONLY ONE.

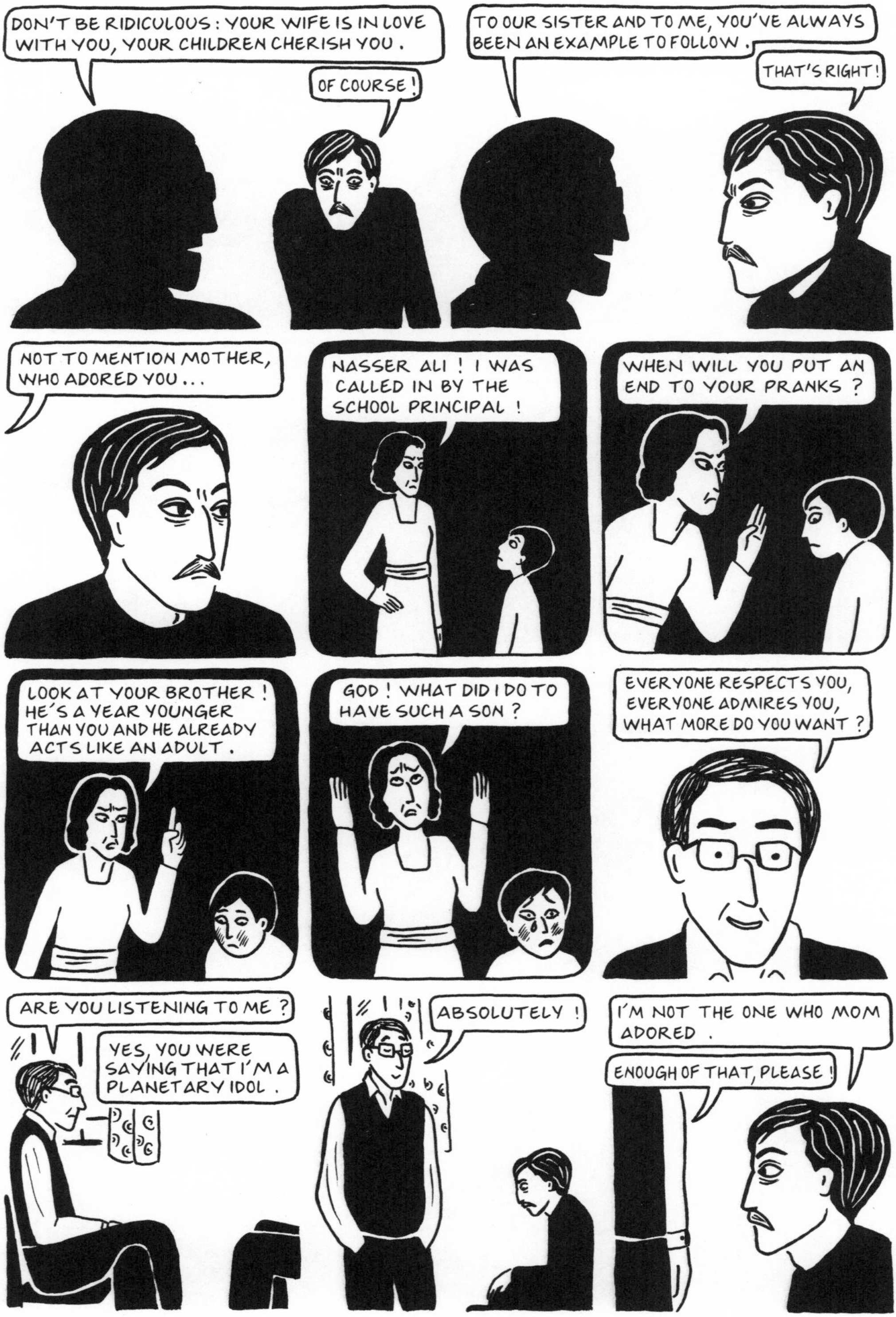
DON'T BE RIDICULOUS : YOUR WIFE IS IN LOVE WITH YOU, YOUR CHILDREN CHERISH YOU .
OF COURSE !
TO OUR SISTER AND TO ME, YOU'VE ALWAYS BEEN AN EXAMPLE TO FOLLOW .
THAT'S RIGHT !
NOT TO MENTION MOTHER, WHO ADORED YOU . . .
NASSER ALI ! I WAS CALLED IN BY THE SCHOOL PRINCIPAL !
WHEN WILL YOU PUT AN END TO YOUR PRANKS ?
LOOK AT YOUR BROTHER ! HE'S A YEAR YOUNGER THAN YOU AND HE ALREADY ACTS LIKE AN ADULT .
GOD ! WHAT DID I DO TO HAVE SUCH A SON ?
EVERYONE RESPECTS YOU, EVERYONE ADMIRES YOU, WHAT MORE DO YOU WANT ?
ARE YOU LISTENING TO ME ?
YES, YOU WERE SAYING THAT I'M A PLANETARY IDOL .
ABSOLUTELY !
I'M NOT THE ONE WHO MOM ADORED .
ENOUGH OF THAT, PLEASE !

*THE SHAH OF IRAN'S FATHER .

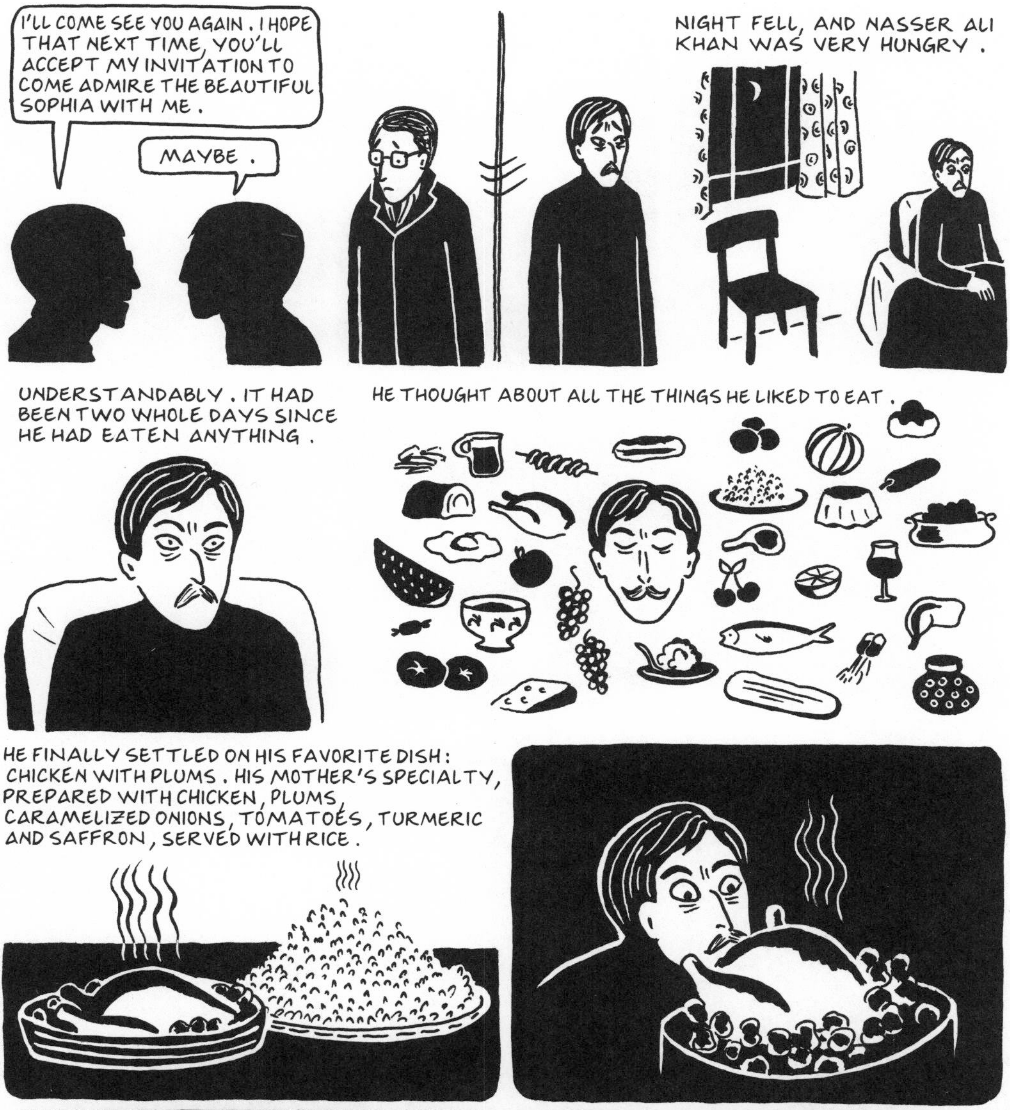
I'LL COME SEE YOU AGAIN. I HOPE THAT NEXT TIME, YOU'LL ACCEPT MY INVITATION TO COME ADMIRE THE BEAUTIFUL SOPHIA WITH ME.
MAYBE.
NIGHT FELL, AND NASSER ALI KHAN WAS VERY HUNGRY.
UNDERSTANDABLY. IT HAD BEEN TWO WHOLE DAYS SINCE HE HAD EATEN ANYTHING.
HE THOUGHT ABOUT ALL THE THINGS HE LIKED TO EAT.
HE FINALLY SETTLED ON HIS FAVORITE DISH: CHICKEN WITH PLUMS. HIS MOTHER'S SPECIALTY, PREPARED WITH CHICKEN, PLUMS, CARAMELIZED ONIONS, TOMATOES, TURMERIC AND SAFFRON, SERVED WITH RICE.

THE THIRD DAY

NOVEMBER 17, 1958

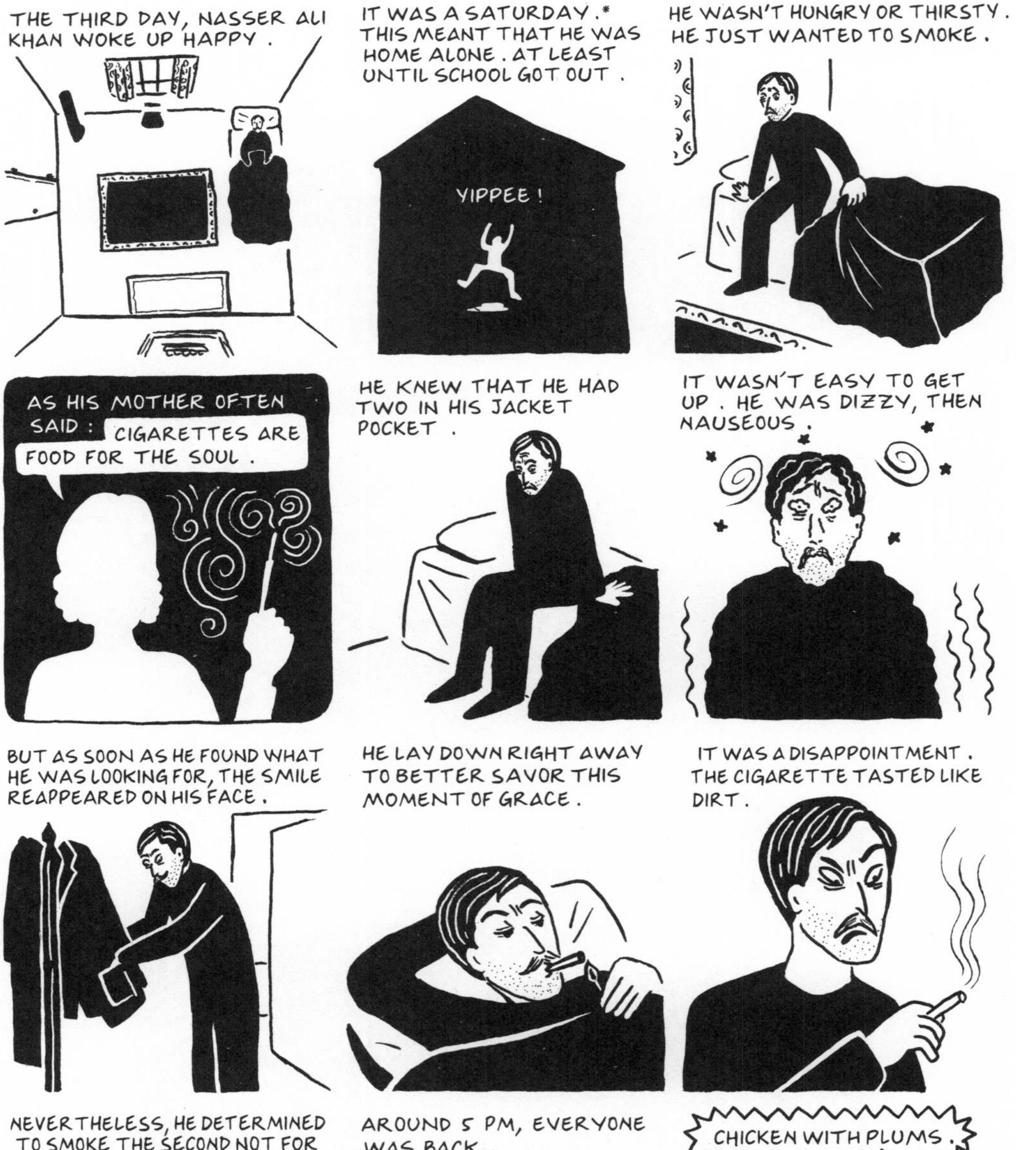
THE THIRD DAY, NASSER ALI KHAN WOKE UP HAPPY.
IT WAS A SATURDAY.* THIS MEANT THAT HE WAS HOME ALONE. AT LEAST UNTIL SCHOOL GOT OUT.
YIPPEE!
HE WASN'T HUNGRY OR THIRSTY. HE JUST WANTED TO SMOKE.
AS HIS MOTHER OFTEN SAID:
CIGARETTES ARE FOOD FOR THE SOUL.
HE KNEW THAT HE HAD TWO IN HIS JACKET POCKET.
IT WASN'T EASY TO GET UP. HE WAS DIZZY, THEN NAUSEOUS.
BUT AS SOON AS HE FOUND WHAT HE WAS LOOKING FOR, THE SMILE REAPPEARED ON HIS FACE.
HE LAY DOWN RIGHT AWAY TO BETTER SAVOR THIS MOMENT OF GRACE.
IT WAS A DISAPPOINTMENT. THE CIGARETTE TASTED LIKE DIRT.
NEVERTHELESS, HE DETERMINED TO SMOKE THE SECOND NOT FOR PLEASURE, BUT OUT OF PRINCIPLE.
AROUND 5 PM, EVERYONE WAS BACK.
MOM! WHAT ARE WE HAVING FOR DINNER?
CHICKEN WITH PLUMS.
NASSER ALI KHAN'S SURPRISE WAS IMMENSE.

*IN IRAN, FRIDAY IS THE HOLIDAY.

FINALLY, THAT NIGHT, HOPING FOR A POSSIBLE RECONCILIATION, NAHID DECIDED TO SERVE A PLATE TO HER HUSBAND.

*IN JANUARY 1936, REZA SHAH FORBADE THE WEARING OF THE VEIL IN IRAN.

45

THE FOURTH DAY

NOVEMBER 18, 1958

NO DAY IN THE SHORT LIFE OF NASSER ALI KHAN WAS MORE BLEAK THAN NOVEMBER 18, 1958.
NOT ONLY HAD HE VICIOUSLY ARGUED WITH HIS WIFE THE DAY BEFORE, BUT TO MAKE MATTERS
WORSE, FOR THE FOUR DAYS THAT HE'D BEEN AWAITING DEATH, ONLY HIS YOUNGEST
DAUGHTER, FARZANEH, HAD DEVOTED HIM A FEW MINUTES OF HER TIME. THE INGRATITUDE
OF HIS THREE OTHER CHILDREN UPSET HIM DEEPLY.

BUT WHEN NIGHT CAME, NASSER ALI KHAN CHANGED HIS MIND. CONVINCED THAT HIS
END WAS NEAR, HE TOLD HIMSELF THAT HE HAD A DUTY TO LEAVE THEM WITH THE
IMAGE OF A GOOD AND GENEROUS MAN. WHICH, AFTER ALL, HE WAS...

NASSER ALI KHAN
DIDN'T LIKE MOZAFFAR
FOR TWO VERY PRECISE
REASONS : FIRST,
BECAUSE HIS WIFE HAD
DECIDED ALONE TO
BRING THIS CHILD INTO
THE WORLD, AND
SECOND, BECAUSE THE
TWO OF THEM HAD
NOTHING IN COMMON ...

MOZAFFAR EMBODIED EVERYTHING THAT NASSER ALI KHAN SCORNED :

DESTINY PROVED NASSER ALI KHAN RIGHT :
INDEED, MOZAFFAR NEVER BECAME THIN, OR AN ARTIST, OR SUICIDAL, OR EVEN MOROSE AND MELANCHOLIC .
IN 1975, HIS TWENTY-SECOND YEAR, MOZAFFAR MARRIED A CERTAIN GILA WHO WAS STUDYING ECONOMICS AND MANAGEMENT WITH HIM .

ALSO IN 1979, AT THE TIME OF THE IRANIAN REVOLUTION, MOZAFFAR WORKED AS A MANAGER IN THE ARMY AND HIS WIFE WAS AN ACCOUNTANT. EVERYTHING WAS GOING WONDERFULLY. GILA HAD FINALLY BEEN ACCEPTED BY HER IN-LAWS.

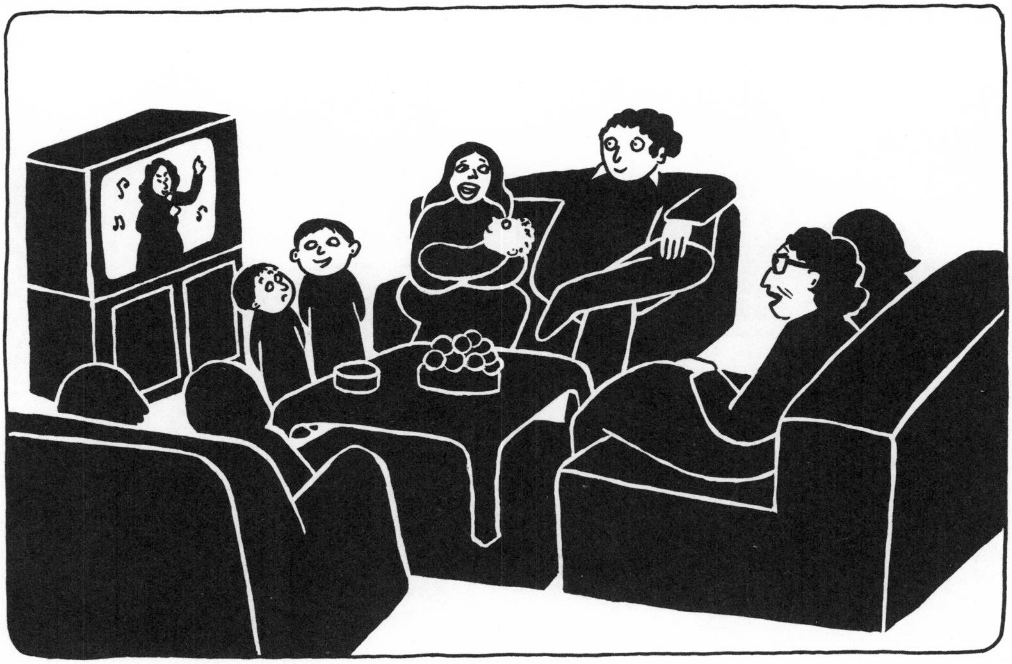

BUT IN 1980 WAR ERUPTED AND THAT WAS THE END OF HAPPINESS.

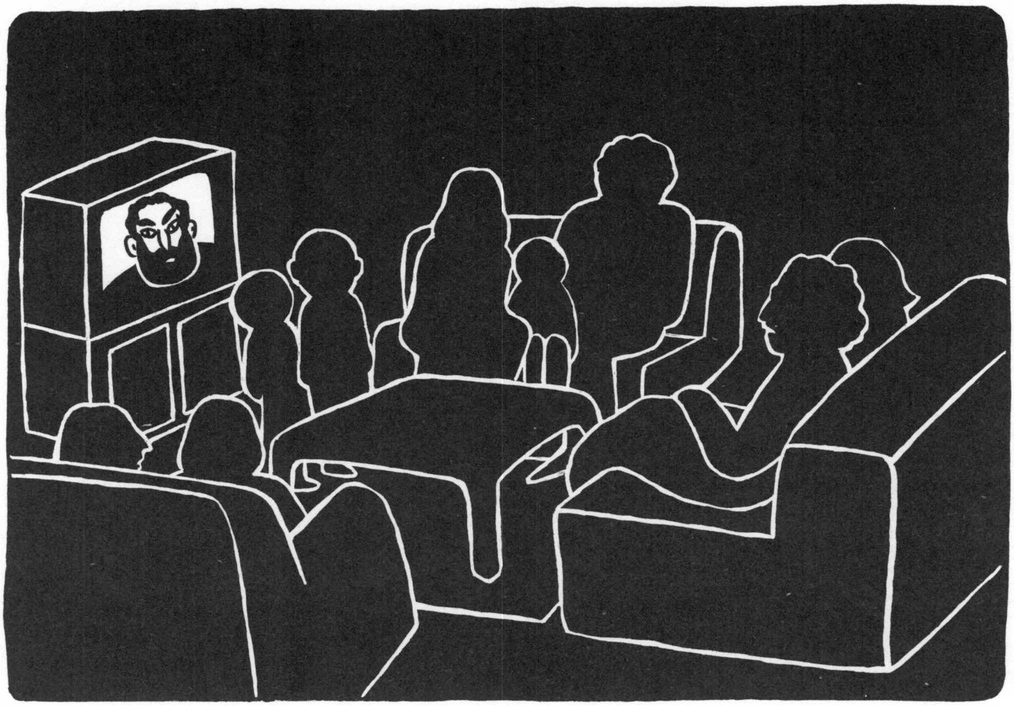

GIVEN THAT MOZAFFAR WORKED FOR THE ARMY, HIS LIFE WAS IN REAL DANGER.
ACCOMPANIED BY HIS FAMILY, HE LEFT IRAN AND SETTLED IN THE UNITED STATES.

EVERYTHING WAS GOING SWIMMINGLY IN THE MOST PERFECT OF WORLDS, EXCEPT...
EXCEPT THAT THEIR CHILDREN HAD SOME SERIOUS WEIGHT PROBLEMS.
MOZAFFAR AND HIS WIFE, ONCE CONSIDERED FAT IN IRAN, LOOKED THIN BESIDE THEM.

APPARENTLY, WHEN THE AUNT IN QUESTION ASKED MOZAFFAR HOW IT WAS POSSIBLE THAT HE WASN'T AWARE OF HIS DAUGHTER'S PREGNANCY, HE ANSWERED THAT IT WAS DIFFICULT TO MAKE OUT AN 8-POUND FETUS IN 400 POUNDS OF MEAT. THE AUNT ADDED : "I AM SURE THAT EVEN MY NIECE DIDN'T KNOW."

NASSER ALI KHAN DIDN'T KNOW HOW LUCKY HE WAS TO DIE FOUR DAYS LATER. IF HE HAD KNOWN THE STORY OF MOZAFFAR AND HIS DAUGHTER, HE WOULD SURELY HAVE CONTRACTED CANCER, WHICH BY ALL ACCOUNTS IS A MUCH SLOWER AND SIGNIFICANTLY MORE PAINFUL WAY TO DIE.

THE FIFTH DAY

NOVEMBER 19, 1958

AT THE DAWN OF THE FIFTH DAY, NASSER ALI KHAN FELT THAT DEATH COULD NO LONGER BE
VERY FAR . HE THOUGHT OF ALL THOSE WHO HAD PASSED AWAY, ALL THOSE WHOM HE HAD
LOVED AND WHO WERE GONE, AS THOUGH THEY HAD NEVER EXISTED .
SUDDENLY, HE CAUGHT SIGHT OF HIS MOTHER IN THE CROWD .

LIKE ALL SONS, NASSER ALI KHAN WAS VERY ATTACHED TO HIS MOTHER . HE
REMEMBERED THE TIME WHEN SHE FELL GRAVELY ILL, FIFTEEN YEARS BEFORE .

OF COURSE HE NEVER TOLD ANYONE ABOUT HIS NIGHTTIME PRAYERS . THEN ONE DAY
HIS MOTHER SUMMONED HIM TO HER ROOM :

59

NASSER ALI KHAN OBEYED . HE BOUGHT THREE DOZEN PACKS OF CIGARETTES AND HANDED THEM OVER TO HIS MOTHER . HE NO LONGER PRAYED FOR HER AND HE PLAYED MUSIC EVERY DAY, FROM SUNRISE TO THE STROKE OF MIDNIGHT .

FROM THE TIME NASSER ALI KHAN STOPPED HIS PRAYERS TO THE NIGHT HIS MOTHER SURRENDERED HER SOUL, EXACTLY SIX DAYS HAD PASSED .

IT SEEMS THAT WHEN THEY DISCOVERED HER BODY, IT WAS ENVELOPED IN A THICK CLOUD OF SMOKE.

THE FUNERAL TOOK PLACE TWO DAYS LATER. THE FAMILY OF THE DECEASED, ALL THE DERVISHES* OF TEHRAN, AS WELL AS THE CLOUD OF SMOKE WERE PRESENT AT THE BURIAL.

THE OPINIONS ON THIS DENSE FOG WERE VERY DIVERGENT:
THE RATIONAL ONES THOUGHT THAT IT WAS THE CIGARETTE SMOKE LEAVING HER BODY. HAVING SAID THIS, THEY WERE NEVER ABLE TO EXPLAIN SCIENTIFICALLY HOW A CADAVER COULD CONTINUE TO EXHALE.
THE DERVISHES, MORE MYSTICAL, HAD A COMPLETELY DIFFERENT OPINION ON THIS SUBJECT:

*SUFI MYSTICS.   ** HEAD OF THE DERVISHES ("GHOTB" IN PERSIAN).

*THE DERVISHES' MOSQUE.

62

*IRANIAN POET (1207–1273). BARD OF MYSTICAL LOVE AND FOUNDER OF THE MOWLAVI ORDER OF SUFIS (KNOWN AS WHIRLING DERVISHES).

FIVE DAYS HAD PASSED AND NASSER ALI KHAN WAS ASKING HIMSELF MANY QUESTIONS :

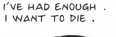

HE CONCLUDED THAT IF DEATH WASN'T KEEPING THEIR APPOINTMENT, IT WAS BECAUSE SOMEONE WAS PRAYING FOR HIM TO GO ON LIVING .

THE NIGHT OF NOVEMBER 19, 1958, A DARK SILENCE REIGNED OVER THE HOUSE.

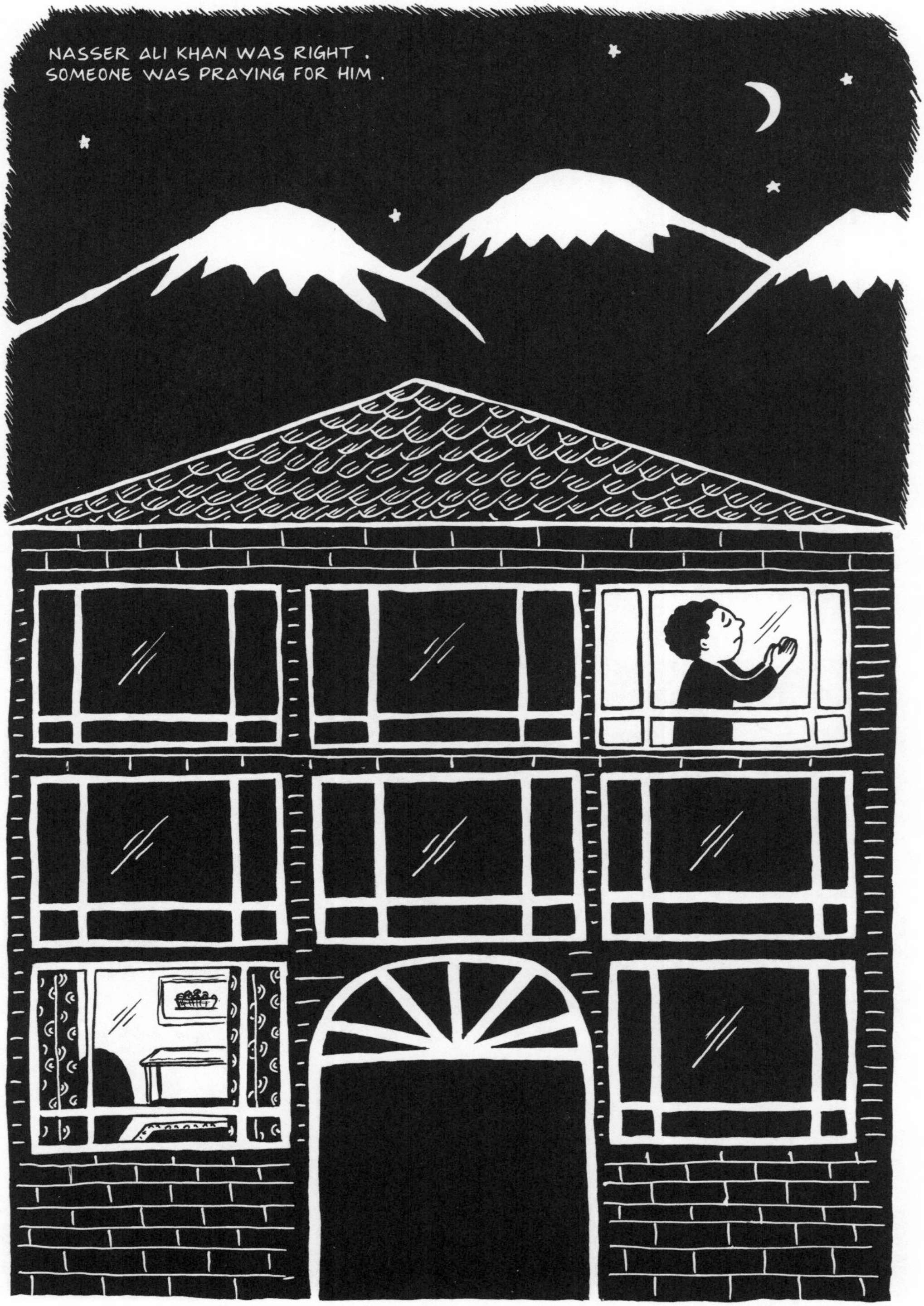
NASSER ALI KHAN WAS RIGHT. SOMEONE WAS PRAYING FOR HIM.

THE SIXTH DAY

NOVEMBER 20, 1958

IN THE COURSE OF THE SIXTH DAY, NASSER ALI KHAN FINALLY SAW AZRAEL, THE ANGEL OF DEATH. EVEN THOUGH HE WAS ANXIOUS TO LEAVE THIS WORLD, HE WAS VERY, VERY SCARED.

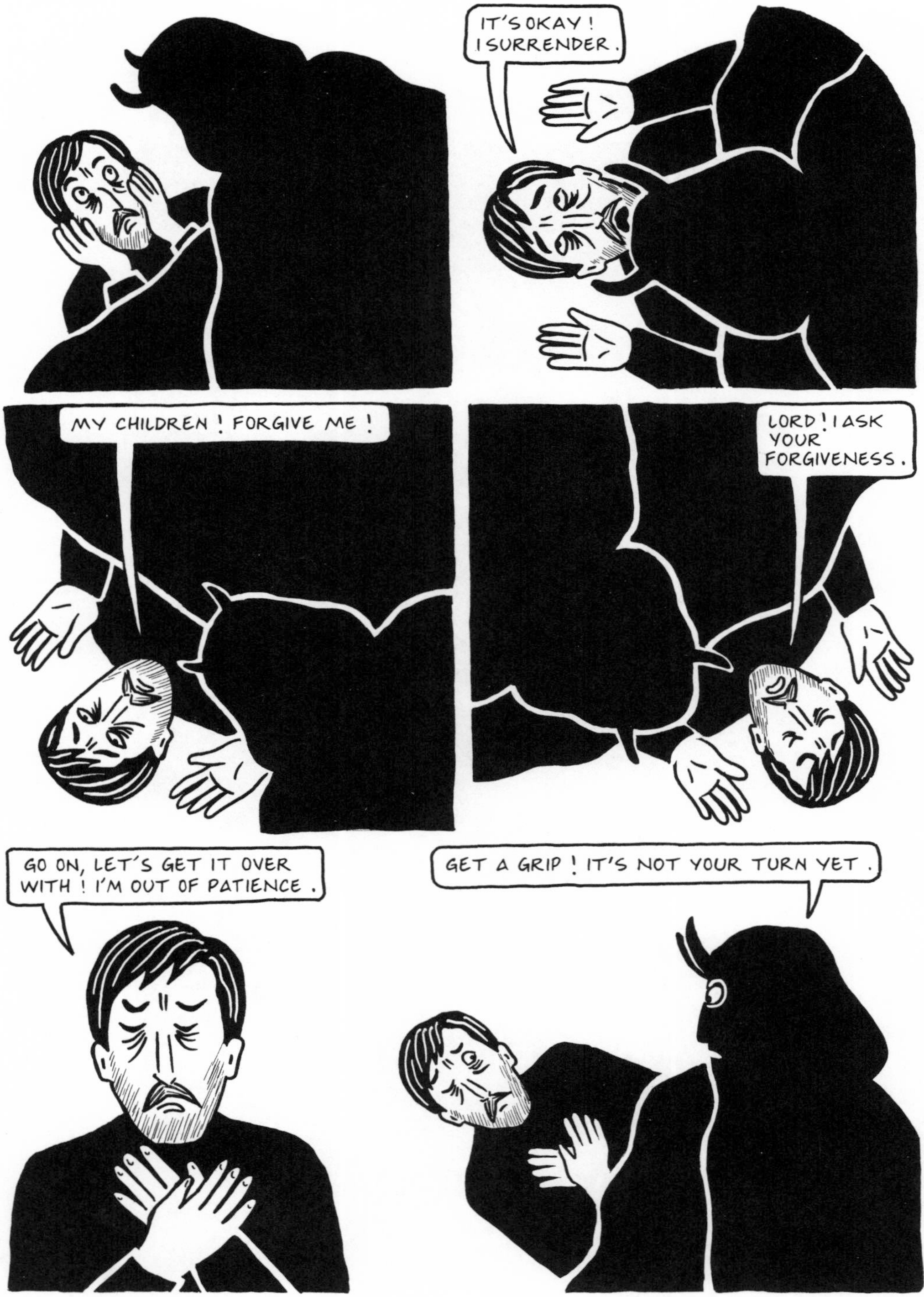
IT'S OKAY! I SURRENDER.
MY CHILDREN! FORGIVE ME!
LORD! I ASK YOUR FORGIVENESS.
GO ON, LET'S GET IT OVER WITH! I'M OUT OF PATIENCE.
GET A GRIP! IT'S NOT YOUR TURN YET.

THE SEVENTH DAY

NOVEMBER 21, 1958

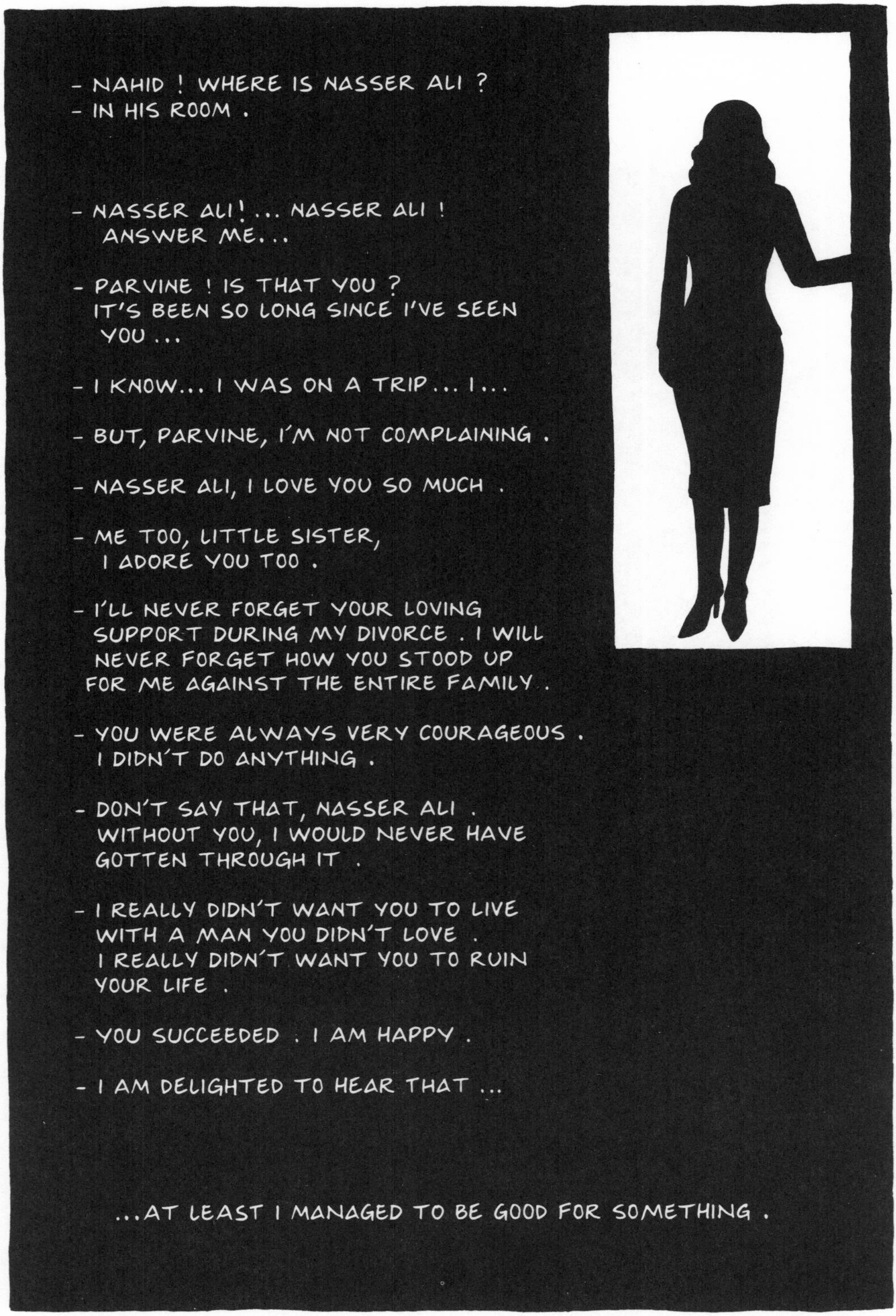
- NAHID ! WHERE IS NASSER ALI ?
- IN HIS ROOM .
- NASSER ALI ! ... NASSER ALI ! ANSWER ME...
- PARVINE ! IS THAT YOU ? IT'S BEEN SO LONG SINCE I'VE SEEN YOU ...
- I KNOW... I WAS ON A TRIP ... I...
- BUT, PARVINE, I'M NOT COMPLAINING .
- NASSER ALI, I LOVE YOU SO MUCH .
- ME TOO, LITTLE SISTER, I ADORE YOU TOO .
- I'LL NEVER FORGET YOUR LOVING SUPPORT DURING MY DIVORCE . I WILL NEVER FORGET HOW YOU STOOD UP FOR ME AGAINST THE ENTIRE FAMILY .
- YOU WERE ALWAYS VERY COURAGEOUS . I DIDN'T DO ANYTHING .
- DON'T SAY THAT, NASSER ALI . WITHOUT YOU, I WOULD NEVER HAVE GOTTEN THROUGH IT .
- I REALLY DIDN'T WANT YOU TO LIVE WITH A MAN YOU DIDN'T LOVE . I REALLY DIDN'T WANT YOU TO RUIN YOUR LIFE .
- YOU SUCCEEDED . I AM HAPPY .
- I AM DELIGHTED TO HEAR THAT ...
...AT LEAST I MANAGED TO BE GOOD FOR SOMETHING .

THE EIGHTH DAY

NOVEMBER 22, 1958

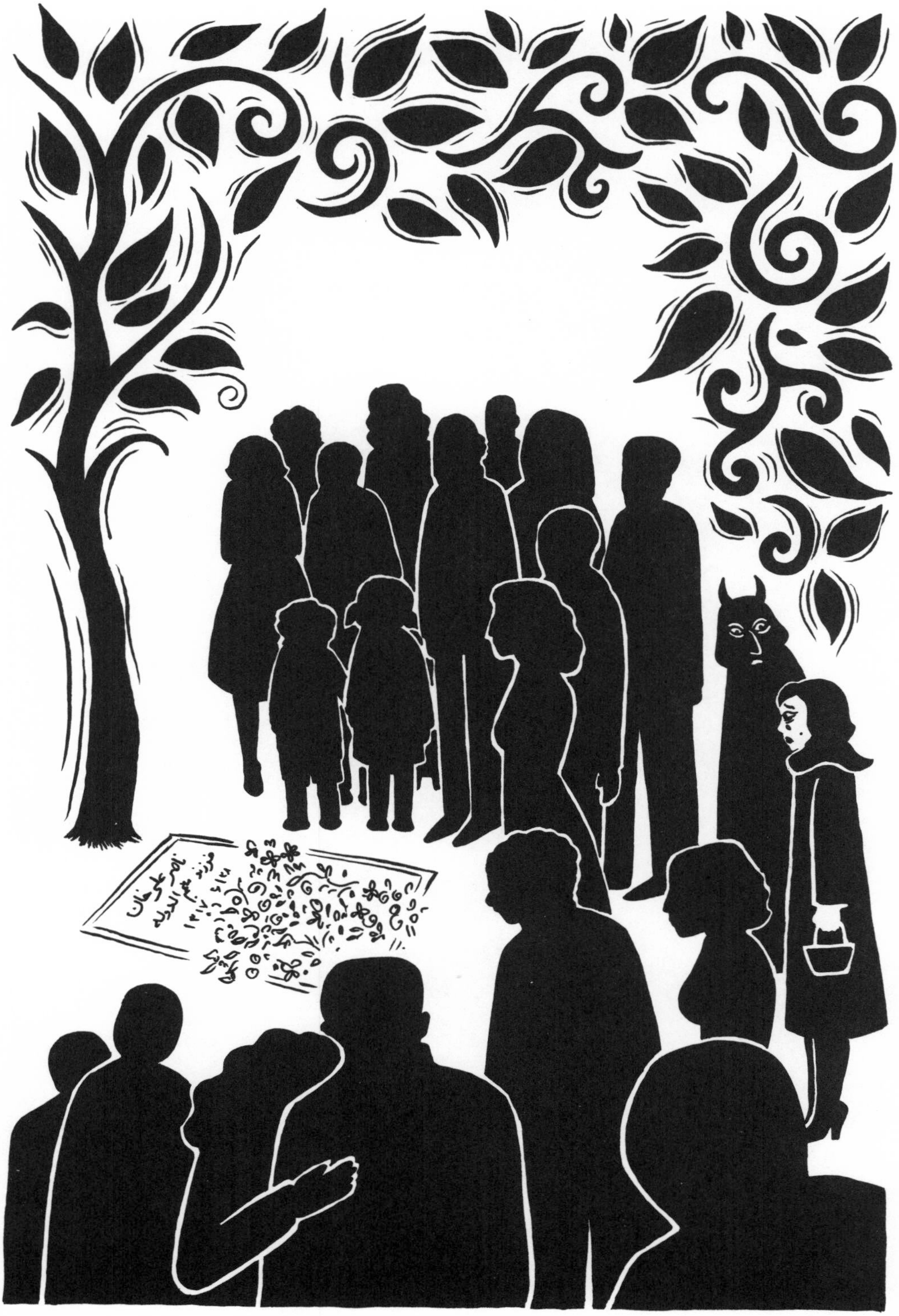
ناصر علی خان

ABOUT THE AUTHOR

Marjane Satrapi was born in 1969 in Rasht, Iran. She now lives in Paris, where she is a regular contributor to magazines and newspapers throughout the world, including *The New Yorker* and *The New York Times*. She is the author of several children's books, *Embroideries,* and her critically acclaimed and internationally bestselling memoir published in two volumes as *Persepolis: The Story of a Childhood* and *Persepolis 2: The Story of a Return. Persepolis* has been translated into more then twenty languages, was a *New York Times* Notable Book, and received the Harvey Award for best American edition of foreign material and an Alex Award from the American Library Association. *Persepolis* is also being made into an animated feature film, cowritten and codirected by Ms. Satrapi, to be distributed by Sony Picture Classics in 2007.